DATE D

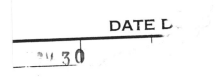

3 0

(

N

William Howard Taft

The President who became Chief Justice

By BILL SEVERN

drawing by Rus Anderson

DAVID McKAY COMPANY, Inc.   NEW YORK

WILLIAM HOWARD TAFT
The President who became Chief Justice

LIBRARY OF CONGRESS CATALOG CARD NUMBER: 72-101963

MANUFACTURED IN THE UNITED STATES OF AMERICA

VAN REES PRESS • NEW YORK

Typography by Charles M. Todd

WILLIAM HOWARD TAFT

The President who became Chief Justice

** CHAPTER **

1

WHEN Will Taft was only seven and in his first year of school, his father wrote: "To be Chief Justice of the United States is more than to be President in my estimation." His father's ambition was for a place on the Supreme Court himself. Will's ambition came much later, but it was the same as his father's. For most of his life, he wanted to be on the Supreme Court.

Along the way, he became a state and Federal judge, Solicitor General of the United States, first governor of the Philippines, Secretary of War, took charge of building the Panama Canal, settled a revolution in Cuba, and was a Yale law professor and a crusader for world peace. He also became the only man in history ever to hold the nation's two highest offices, first as President and then as Chief Justice, and to prove to his own satisfaction that his father had been right and that it was better to be Chief Justice than President.

His grandfather, Peter Rawson Taft, had been a county judge in Vermont and during most of Will's school years his father, Alphonso Taft, was a judge of Ohio's superior court, but as a boy Will never guessed he would carry the tradition of being a judge into the third generation. His own thoughts were more about winning ball games. Among the neighborhood boys who played baseball in an abandoned quarry down the hill from his home he was considered a pretty good second baseman, quick at stopping line drives and at throwing to first, and a slugger at bat. But he was slow running bases because he was fat.

Even when he was a baby, seven weeks after he was born on September 15, 1857, his mother wrote, "He is very large of his age and grows fat every day. . . . He spreads his hands to anyone who will take him and his face is wreathed with smiles at the slightest provocation." All his life, Will kept both his fat and his good nature. Yet he could put up a fight when he had to.

There were two wars in his childhood. One was the war of neighborhood gangs, carried on between his pals and boys from other parts of Cincinnati's suburbs. When invaders came up over the hill where he lived, Will was the leader of the defending young warriors. The other war in his childhood was the nation's. He was four when the Civil War began, too young to understand what it was about, but some things remained vivid memories.

His father, Alphonso, had first met Lincoln while in Washington as a lawyer appearing before the Supreme Court. Later he was in the hectic wartime capital again when Lincoln issued the Emancipation Proclamation, and he told his sons of that. Alphonso had been one of the Northerners who broke away from the dying Whig party over the issue of extending slavery into the new states. Out of informal meetings such as those held in his Cincinnati law office had come the beginnings of Ohio's Republican party.

All through the Civil War, Will's home filled with its echoes, and he sensed its tensions and anxieties. His father was out making speeches, selling war bonds, recruiting troops; his mother was busy with hospital care for the wounded. Will never forgot the day after the war ended when his father called the children into the parlor to tell them Lincoln was dead. From the city below, through the day and into the night, he heard the slow and mournful tolling of church bells.

But despite the war, Will's first years were given more to the simple pleasures of a city boy in what were still country surroundings. On both sides of his family there was a Yankee heritage that went back to the beginnings of America. He grew up as a New Englander in Ohio, a boy who lived on a hilltop in what was then suburban Mount Auburn, above the noisy big city of Cincinnati. He had a country boyhood in a house ruled by stern traditions closer to the rock-ribbed East than to the booming new freedoms of the Midwest.

From his Grandfather Peter, who had been transplanted from Vermont to live with the family in Cincinnati, Will learned about the Robert Taft who had first come from England as a carpenter in the late 1600's to settle in Massachusetts, and of other ancestors who had fought the Indians, and served in the Revolution. As a fourteen-year-old boy himself, Grandpa Peter had moved with the family across the granite hills from Massachusetts in 1799, in a midwinter journey to settle in Windham County, Vermont, walking most of the eighty miles through the snow, driving the family cow.

When Will's father was old enough for college, he had walked from the Vermont farm all the way to New Haven to enter Yale, and each summer had walked home again to help on the farm, until he graduated with honors in 1833. He had taught school in Connecticut while he studied law, and as a young lawyer had headed West to seek a place of opportunity, arriving in Cincinnati without a dollar to spare. By thrift and hard work, Alphonso had become a prospering leader of the Ohio bar, active in civic affairs and Republican politics, and was the first of the Tafts to achieve state and national prominence.

Alphonso's first wife, Fanny Phelps, from his home village in Vermont, had died in 1852, leaving him with two young sons to raise, nine-year-old Charles and six-year-old Peter. Eighteen months later, after a whirlwind courtship, he married Louise Torrey, whom he had met through friends in New Haven during a visit there. He took her back to Cincinnati to the big square house on Mount Auburn to live with her Taft in-laws, to mother his first wife's sons, and to become Will's mother. She and Alphonso had both wanted a daughter when Will was born, but in the following years she had two more sons, Henry and Horace, to make it a household of five brothers before there finally was a sister, Frances Louise.

Will's Grandpa Torrey, his mother's father, had been a well-to-do Boston merchant before he retired to a farm at Millbury, Massachusetts, and the boys spent some of their summers there. The Torreys had come to the Massachusetts Bay Colony even before the first Tafts, and Will's grandfather was a stern but loving old Yankee who would stand for no nonsense. Sharp-tongued and determined, he was ready to apply a stinging if elderly hand to the seat of the pants of any young Taft who misbehaved. When the boys visited Millbury, Grandpa Torrey saw to it that they earned their keep by clearing fields of stones and by cutting wood. They rose at dawn, went to bed at dusk, minded their manners, and spent Sundays in quiet and unbroken religious devotion.

There was strict discipline in Will's Mount Auburn home, too, if not as strict as at Millbury. His father constantly stressed the virtues of hard work, thrift and integrity, and although the Tafts were able to afford hired help, the boys were assigned house and garden tasks as part of their family duty. But there was nothing grim about Will's childhood; he was surrounded with love and security.

Shorn of his long blond curls at the age of four, he grew up a healthy outdoor boy, taught to play ball and to wrestle and swim by his older brothers, whom he never thought of as half-brothers. When he started public grammar school at the age of six, he could read and spell but he was poor at first in writing and arithmetic. His father and mother put him to work on extra daily lessons at home and made him understand they would never accept anything less than his very best.

Before he finished grammar school he was at the head of his class and had won a medal for scholarship with a 95 average and perfect test scores in arithmetic, history, grammar, geography, composition and spelling. Even with all his studying he still found time to play ball and to help defend the neighborhood's honor in fights with rival gangs. Dismayed by the youthful gang wars, his mother tried to make him more of a young gentleman by sending him to dancing school. Somewhat to her surprise, he enjoyed it and became a good dancer, but also went right on fighting.

From the time he was eight until he was fifteen his father was judge of the superior court and the first stirrings of what was to be Will's strongest ambition came from visits to the courtroom. On those nights when his father brought home briefs to study, working for hours at the flat table that was his desk while Will did his homework nearby, they often talked about the law. His father delighted in telling him of the romantic early history of law, when medieval courts had grown out of the trials by combat of men battling with clubs to settle their differences, before they learned to make rules for the orderly respect of rights and property. Will's love for the law's traditions began in those evenings with his father; in later years he couldn't remember when he had made the decision to become a lawyer himself—it was something gradually taken for granted between father and son.

Will had an early lesson, too, in the public rage that an unpopular court ruling can arouse, when his father became the center of a fight over religious instruction in the schools. A Catholic group petitioned Cincinnati's school board to ban the use of the Protestant version of the Bible, and when a Protestant group filed suit to keep the board from acting, the controversy had all of Cincinnati taking sides. Since most of the city's Republicans then were Protestants and most Democrats were Catholics, it became a political as well as a religious fight. Two of the three superior court judges who heard the case ruled that the school board had no right to end religious instruction or to remove the Protestant Bible from the schools.

But Will's father, although both Protestant and Republican,

believed the law clearly was on the side of separation of church and state. He filed a dissenting opinion, declaring that the school board not only had the right but also the legal obligation to keep sectarian religious instruction and Bible reading out of the public schools, and the Ohio Supreme Court upheld him and overturned the majority ruling.

The decision flamed into headlines across the country, and in Ohio there was a more immediate fury. Alphonso was publicly denounced as immoral, ungodly and no better than an atheist for removing the Bible from the schools; privately he was called a traitor to his own Republican party and to his social class.

Will and the whole Taft family felt the sting of this furor for a time. Actually the Tafts were strong churchgoers. His father had become a trustee of the Unitarian church where Will regularly went to Sunday school. But even that was held against them by some members of older Protestant sects who looked with deep suspicion on what they considered the liberal Unitarian religion. The issue badly hurt Will's father politically, but he later told Will he never regretted his court decision; he took pride in it as the most important opinion he had written during his career as a judge.

When Will was thirteen, in the fall of 1870, he began his first year at Woodward High School in downtown Cincinnati. It was a mile's steep walk in each direction from his hilltop home, which his parents considered good exercise. Woodward had a reputation as one of the first public schools in the Midwest to offer adequate college preparation; students who went there were informed that in exchange for such free education they either worked or got out. Its standards were so high it wasn't unusual for two-fifths of a class to fail.

School began at eight-thirty in the morning. Will's subjects were Latin, Greek, mathematics, history, literature and elocution, with no breaks for study periods or even for lunch. Students were dismissed at one-thirty in the afternoon with enough homework to keep them busy until the next day.

Woodward was strictly a place for learning, with clubs, school sports or other activities unheard of, and lingering about the grounds after school for any reason was forbidden. Will and his friends called it The Bastille, because the high iron fence that surrounded the school suggested the infamous French prison.

He was such a model student and got such high marks for good conduct as well as class work that he might have been thoroughly hated if he hadn't also been so good-natured. He already had the deep laughter that was to be well known in later years and the ability to accomplish a lot of intense hard work without seeming to take anything seriously, especially himself. He was popular and well liked and he called it "luck" when his grades averaged in the 90's during his first two years at Woodward. The third year his average dropped to 86 and he was taken to task by his parents and by one of his teachers for being "lazy." But as a senior he was second highest in his class, with a final all-subject average of 91.

There were no school teams at Woodward, but in the afternoons he still played baseball, took up bowling, and gained a reputation as an amateur wrestler. Among his high school pals was Rufus Smith, who lived nearby. Will spent hours at his house, the two of them going through old volumes of *Harper's Weekly* when they had nothing better to do. But Rufus sometimes suspected Will was more interested in his pretty sister Sallie than he was in *Harper's*.

Will's oldest brother, Charles, had become a young man of the world with independent means because of an inheritance of $50,000 from his mother's family. After graduating from Yale and gaining law degrees at Columbia, Heidelberg and the Sorbonne, he returned to Cincinnati to practice law and serve a term in the Ohio legislature. The biggest social event in Will's young life was in December, 1873, when Charles married Annie Sinton, the only daughter of one of Ohio's wealthiest men. Charles soon turned his attention to journalism and with his father-in-law consolidated two newspapers into the *Cincinnati Times-Star,* of which he became editor and publisher, on his way also to becoming a multimillionaire.

Charles had set a high goal for Will with the honors he had won at Yale, and his next oldest brother, Peter, had graduated from Yale highest in his class. When Peter received his scholarship awards, Will went with his father to New Haven to see the university he had heard about all his life and to sit proudly in the audience. His father had become a member of the Yale Corporation and it was taken for granted that Will would go there. When he graduated from Woodward High in 1874 at the age of seventeen the time finally came for him to uphold the family tradition. That he would lead his class at Yale also was taken for granted, by everyone but Will.

** CHAPTER **

2

WHEN William Howard Taft had been elected President of the United States, thirty years after he left Yale, the influence of his college years was still so strong that he said, "I love Yale as I love my mother."

He was not quite eighteen when he arrived on the New Haven campus in the fall of 1874, a tall 225-pound, blue-eyed and fair-haired boy from Cincinnati, who immediately discovered his scholarly triumphs at Woodward High meant nothing against the keener competion at Yale, and that "a fellow can work hard all the time and still not have perfect marks." He wrote his father, "You expect great things of me, but you mustn't be disappointed if I don't come up to your expectations."

Will shared a Farnham Hall room with George Edwards from Kentucky. He had to supply his own personal furnishings, which worried him because he had gone five dollars over his allowance to buy a study lamp and the kerosene to burn in it, pay for his laundry and ten tickets for taking baths, and had splurged a whole dollar in dues for the freshman boating club. Expected to send home a strict daily accounting, he tried to soften paternal wrath by writing, "I have spent no money for candy or fruit as you see."

Complaining about having to get out of bed at six-thirty so he had time to look over his lessons before breakfast, prayer service, and his first class at eight, he described his life as one of recitations and "grubbing until three o'clock, gymnasium half an hour, study until five, recitation, supper. . . . Then I work till ten, sometimes eleven." Chapel services bored him and the wooden seats were so uncomfortably hard that he joked about not being able to fall asleep and being doomed to listen to the "driest sermons I ever heard."

But he found no temptation to sleep in his classrooms, with the level of mind-challenging work so "astonishing" he had to "make a rush every day to keep in front." His freshman class was divided into sections according to merit and he placed in the first division, along with another Cincinnati boy, his pal, Howard Hollister. Yale was still a citadel of New England conservatism, although somewhat less rigidly so than in his father's time. Such "frills" had been added to the basic classical education as a school of science and a school of fine arts, and undergraduates were allowed some choice, if not much, in deciding what courses to take.

Will drew giants among his professors. Thomas Thatcher taught him Latin, and he studied rhetoric under Professor Cyrus Northrop, later President of the University of Minnesota. He learned English literature from Henry Augustin Beers, a renowned authority. But the man who had the most influence in shaping his mind to views he would hold all his life was Professor William Graham Sumner. Half a century later Taft still felt Sumner "had more to do with stimulating my mental activities than anyone under whom I studied."

Sumner, a Yale graduate himself, had studied in England, Germany and Switzerland, and had become an active Episcopalian minister before returning to Yale as its professor of political and social sciences. Still in his thirties, he was to be an inspiring teacher at Yale for forty years, as well as an outstanding economist and sociologist. He was a convincing advocate of free trade, a foe of American imperialism, a stinging critic of big government, and a crusader for civil service reform. Most of all, Sumner was an ardent preacher of the laissez-faire policy of letting the nation's economy take care of itself while the government kept its hands off.

As a freshman, Will showed little of the dazzling brilliance his older brothers had displayed at Yale and his father was worried by reports that he was becoming popular on the campus. "I doubt that such popularity is consistent with high scholarship," his father wrote, but Will took the stern advice from home in his stride and didn't let it keep him entirely locked up with his books.

During the annual Freshman Rush, he became something of a class hero. Each year sophomores challenged freshmen to what usually turned into a free-for-all that left both sides bruised, mud-smeared and with ripped clothing. When the faculty tried to prevent the class warfare by warning that such activities had become frowned upon, it was Will who rallied the freshmen with a cry that the Class of '78 should not be the first to run from the sophs. He waded into the fray, and according to reports, tossed six of the enemy into the mud before an exhausted truce was called.

With that triumph behind him, he gained added campus glory as the champion wrestler of the class, after a bout in which he pinned the sophomore champion, E. C. Cook, to the mat. He also became a skilled rower and was asked to join the Yale crew, but his father would have none of that, nor would he agree to let Will join the football team, or play the game of baseball he loved. Alphonso condemned such college activities as a childish waste of time and sharply reminded Will that his sole reason for being at Yale was to get an education.

More pleasing to his father was the fact that he was drawing attention as an orator and that he had taken a decided interest in politics. When his father made an unsuccessful bid in the spring of 1875 to become Republican nominee for Governor of Ohio, Will found it hard to be at Yale and out of the thick of political battle at home.

The family's good friend, Rutherford Hayes, had announced that he did not want a third term as governor, so Alphonso campaigned for the nomination. But the old issue of his court decision against religious instruction in public schools was raised against him. Meanwhile, supporters were convincing Hayes that another term as governor might be a good stepping-stone to the White House. Hayes had encouraged Alphonso to enter the contest, so he announced that even if the Republicans nominated him he would refuse to run for governor. But at the state party convention, Alphonso withdrew in favor of Hayes and moved to make Hayes' nomination unanimous. Hayes was extremely grateful to him for helping him return to the governor's chair, a place he soon would leave to become President.

Will was badly disappointed that his father did not become Ohio's governor, but during his sophomore year at Yale his father did become outgoing President Grant's Secretary of War. The Grant administration, shaken by one scandal after another, was caught in a new one when General William Belknap, who had been Secretary of War, resigned under fire after being impeached on charges of taking $25,000 as a bribe to put through an Army trading post contract. Anxious to put someone of "unblemished reputation" in his place, Grant named Alphonso Taft in March, 1876.

It wasn't easy for Will to keep his mind on his studies while his father was at the center of the political storm in Washington, with the unhappy task of trying to halt corruption, curb patronage and cut military expenses. Alphonso had little chance to prove what he could do as Secretary of War because within three months there was another cabinet shake-up and Grant made him Attorney General. That was more in line with Alphonso's judicial and legal training, but in the bungling last days of the Grant administration his task became mostly one of trying to help Republicans hold the White House against the tide of public protest that threatened to bring Democrats back to power for the first time since the Civil War.

Will had an inside view, through his father's eyes, of the Presidency, the cabinet and official Washington. During the hot summer of political debate, he also had a revealing view of the campaign that led to one of the most disputed elections in the nation's history. Opposed to Republican Hayes in the 1876 battle for the Presidency was New York's Democratic Governor Samuel J. Tilden, who had helped rebuild the shattered Democratic party and who had become "the Great Reformer" by smashing the Boss Tweed Ring and other gangs of political corruption.

When the November election came Will was back at Yale as a junior, but like the rest of the nation the campus was torn by the dispute over the election results. Tilden had been chosen President by an overwhelming majority of voters. He had won a quarter of a million more popular votes than Hayes. But the electoral votes were in question, especially in three Southern states where Republican forces of Reconstruction still controlled the election machinery.

There was fear of anarchy, rioting, or even another Civil War as both Republicans and Democrats used trickery, bribery and intimidation to produce two sets of conflicting votes from the disputed states. For an agonizing four months nobody knew who would take charge of the government. Congress, given the task of deciding the election, was politically at odds, the Constitution was vague about the counting procedure involved, and for the first time there seemed to be no clear rule for continuing the Presidency. Finally an electoral commission was named to make the decision. And it was Will's father, as Grant's Attorney General, who helped draft the bill creating the commission.

It was a commission that refused, by a strictly party vote, to make any real investigation of the disputed returns. By the same Republican party rule, it named Hayes the next President by one electoral vote. Tilden was politically outmaneuvered in what had been a dirty fight on both sides; in future years many historians would agree that the election had been stolen from him.

Even at the time, Will had serious doubts. As a Yale junior he questioned the decision, although his father had helped create the electoral commission and, in so doing, had helped make a man President who was both a Republican and a close family friend. In a campus speech on "The Vitality of the Democratic Party," Will traced the party's history and rebirth, and after praising Jefferson and Jackson as its founding fathers, declared that it had come before the country and made such a fight "as to create doubt in many an honest mind as to whether the decision against it was according to equity and justice."

Will didn't call the decision wrong or imply that he was sorry to see Hayes chosen as President, but he did make it clear that he thought there were two sides to the question. He called for "a close watch" over "the encroachments of the general government" and said that the Democrats had "an everlasting foundation on which to base . . . party faith."

He was busy, too, in his junior year winning a campus political battle of his own as class orator. "I have not done so well this term as I did last," Will admitted in a letter to his father. Even though he had slipped a little in some subjects, however, he had managed to win a prize for math. When he lost another junior year award he was trying to win, he wrote his mother, "I don't care because father knows I worked hard."

His brother, Henry, arrived at Yale during Will's junior year and became his roommate. But as a senior Will lived in Old South College. While he was still calm and easygoing most of the time, the burden of study sometimes made him lose his temper. One night two friends from across the hall interrupted his studying by lounging around and telling jokes; he finally exploded and drove them out by hurling books, a lamp and a chair at them.

He took great pride in being elected to the senior honor

society, Skull and Bones. But when the final senior marks were posted, his father had to be satisfied with Will's coming out second best. His good friend, Clarence Kelsey, beat him by a few points and became class valedictorian. Will was second in his class of one hundred and thirty-two students and was salutatorian at the commencement in June, 1878.

His commencement oration had little to do with its impressive title: "The Professional and Political Prospects of the College Graduate." He was not quite twenty-one and his speech tracing the evils that afflicted the nation was filled with heavy-handed platitudes. But he did shock some of Yale's predominantly Republican parents, including his own, with the statement that the Republican party had "lost its grip upon the affections of the people."

Thirty years later, when he amusingly recalled his graduation from Yale, speaking then as the new Republican President of the United States, Taft said that as seniors in 1878 he and the others thought "we knew a great deal more than our fathers did." It took the years after "we stepped down out of the dignity of that last year of college to convince us that we were not altogether indispensable to the growth of civilization," he said. "At least, if the world needed us, if the world was yearning for us, the world was able to conceal it."

✳✳ CHAPTER ✳✳

3

YALE would have welcomed Will Taft back to study for a law degree and with his scholarship honors and family connections he might have gone to almost any other great university law school. Instead he decided to stay home in Cincinnati where his friends were and where he expected to make his law career. He chose Cincinnati Law School, which later became part of the city's university but was still a small and independent institution in 1878.

Classes were held two hours each morning in the old Mercantile Library Building in the heart of the city, where Taft had gone to dancing school as a boy. He and sixty other students crowded into a third-floor room heated only by an iron stove to hear distinguished attorneys deliver lectures on the broad principles of law. Despite its small size, the school had a fine reputation for giving a thorough grounding in legal theory, but students were expected to get their practical knowledge working in a law office. Taft did his law reading at his father's office, where he also performed routine legal chores.

Although he didn't openly rebel against his father's constant driving of him, he calmly resisted being pushed too hard. He meant to enjoy life and take the future as it came. With his old friend, Rufus Smith, and his Yale pal "Hol" Hollister, who had come back to law school with him, he took to dining at the city's best restaurants, making the rounds of Cincinnati's German beer gardens, and seeing most of the shows that came to town. He liked musical comedies best because of their catchy popular songs and pretty girls. But when it came to attractive young ladies, he had discovered that Cincinnati itself abounded in them and "nowhere . . . will you find girls as pretty, as interesting, as stylish, and as fresh."

Considered handsome and fun to be with, "that adorable Will Taft" stirred quite a flutter of feminine heartbeats and matrimonial hopes, but he seldom dated the same girl twice in a row and marriage then was about the last thing on his mind. When he first met Nellie Herron, the winter after he started law school, he liked her but neither of them was overcome by love at first sight. Their mothers were good friends, their fathers had been associated as lawyers for forty years, and Nellie's sister was a schoolmate of Will's sister. Somehow he had never noticed Nellie until he met her at a party given by his brother, Charles, and took her bobsledding in the moonlight down Mount Auburn's hill.

Nellie's father, John Herron, had been a college friend of Benjamin Harrison, a former law partner and intimate friend of Rutherford Hayes, and like Taft's father was among Cincinnati's leading attorneys and most prominent Republicans. Christened Helen but seldom called that, Nellie was small, dark-haired, slim-waisted, and had her own court of admirers at eighteen. Gay, free-spirited, somewhat Bohemian, she mildly shocked some of her friends by enjoying an occasional cigarette or a few glasses of beer, and was a very independent young lady who refused to let her femininity hide the fact that she had a good mind. Her interests were intellectual, and her opinions about music, literature, philosophy and politics were outspoken.

She wasn't about to be swept off her feet by Will Taft, nor did he show any immediate desire to do the sweeping. The year before they met she had been a guest for a week at the White House and had told her friend, President Hayes, that she wouldn't mind at all if she someday became the nation's First Lady. After the night of the bobsledding party, she and Taft met now and then, but it was a year before he took her to a formal dance, and she noted in her diary afterwards that he seemed so indifferent she wondered why he had bothered. It took five more years of gradually falling in love to bring them to marriage.

He had become a very busy young man. In addition to his law studies, he had taken a job as a part-time reporter, covering the city's courts for the *Cincinnati Commercial.* Making the daily rounds of the courtrooms, writing about everything from waterfront crime to complicated Federal cases, he gained a down-to-earth education in the law at work, and did so well as a reporter the newspaper's editor offered him a permanent job at double the average pay if he would give up law for journalism. But Taft turned it down, although he continued to write for the paper. The law was still his ambition and in May, 1880, he went to the state capital at Columbus, passed his examination by a committee of judges, and was admitted to the bar.

His father had decided to make another attempt in 1879 to seek the Republican nomination for Governor of Ohio. Again, it was a losing battle, but the young Taft went into the wards of Cincinnati to win state convention delegates for his father, and had his first direct experience in the rough and tumble of machine politics and the battling of bosses for power. In 1880 he also joined in the Ohio Republican campaigning for the election of James Garfield as President and made his first public political speeches at Garfield rallies.

As a reporter for the *Commercial,* he had become a good friend of the county's young prosecuting attorney, Miller Outcault. Outcault had launched a crusade against a noted criminal lawyer, Tom Campbell, who was charged with using political influence, bribery and jury tampering as well as courtroom eloquence to help a long list of accused men escape punishment for crimes ranging from theft to murder. Nobody had been able to prove anything against Campbell, but Taft was among those who believed he was as crooked as his fees were high. When Campbell blocked the conviction of Cy Hoffman, a city auditor accused of embezzling $12,000, Outcault charged that his own boss, county prosecutor Samuel Drew, had been in on the deal.

Taft wrote a revealing series of reports for the *Commercial* that backed Outcault's charges. When the next election came, the voters threw Drew out of office and put Outcault in as the new county prosecutor. He immediately appointed Taft as assistant prosecutor of Hamilton County, which was the beginning of his career in public office that would span the next half-century.

As soon as he took office in January, 1881, he and Outcault renewed the crusade against Campbell, crime and corruption in Cincinnati. As a crime-fighting assistant district attorney, Taft made impassioned courtroom pleas in frequent battles with Campbell for jury decisions. Cincinnati's rough waterfront area produced occasional crimes of violence, including murder, but most of Taft's cases were the more routine prosecution of an array of petty thieves and other disorderly characters who disturbed the city's peace and quiet. What he gained most from it was excellent practice in trial and courtroom work, but it also brought him considerable personal publicity which kept his name before the public and in the minds of Republican politicians.

"Like every well-trained Ohio man, I always had my plate right side up when offices were falling," he said years afterwards, writing candidly about his early rise in politics. "I got my political pull, first, through my father's prominence; then through the fact that I was hail-fellow-well-met with all of the political people of the city. . . . I also worked hard in my ward."

But Taft hardly expected the fat political plum that dropped into his plate when Chester A. Arthur became President after Garfield was assassinated. Taft's father had been angling for a diplomatic appointment and President Arthur called Alphonso to Washington late in 1881 to tell him he was about to be named the nation's new minister to Austria-Hungary, and to surprise him with the added information that there was also a Presidential appointment in line for his son, as Collector of Internal Revenue for the First District, with headquarters in Cincinnati, one of the most tax-productive revenue districts in the country because of the large number of whiskey distilleries in Ohio and Kentucky.

When Taft's appointment was announced a liquor industry trade journal, eager to win his good influence, glowingly described the new Collector of Internal Revenue as a "large, handsome and fair" young man of twenty-four, "with the build of a Hercules and the sunny disposition of an innocent child." He was, the journal said, "the personal choice of the President and the youngest collector in the United States."

As Taft soon discovered, he also was a pawn in a game of politics being played from the White House. President Arthur, anxious to strengthen his own faction within the Republican party, had asked his political lieutenants in Ohio to suggest someone to replace the man who had been in charge of the revenue office. Taft was recommended as a young man who hadn't been in politics long enough to make many enemies and one who could be expected to serve the administration's best interests.

Taft took command of the revenue district in March, 1882, while his father and mother went off to Vienna and diplomatic duties at the court of Emperor Franz Josef. He quickly lost most of his "sunny disposition" and also whatever innocence he still had about the reasons for his appointment. From his first week in the big office overlooking Cincinnati's Fountain Square, he thoroughly hated the job. There was little to interest him in the drudgery of tax collections, detailed financial reports, and complicated governmental paper work that kept him long hours at his desk with the feeling that he was really accomplishing nothing.

He found that his staff, like that of most government agencies in the 1800's, was made up of political hacks and that he was expected to replace them with others no more competent but more deserving of favors as President Arthur's supporters. Taft finally balked when a former Republican Congressman, seeking reelection, bluntly ordered him to fire some of his best men and to appoint others loyal to the President's party faction. When Taft refused, he was informed that the request had come from the President himself.

Both he and his father were under obligation to the President and to refuse a political favor when the administration needed strong backing in Ohio might injure his father's career as well as his own. But while Taft had been willing to go along with minor changes "for the good of the party," he couldn't stomach such a bold patronage grab. He wrote his father, explaining the situation. The men he was being asked to remove, he said, were "perhaps the best men in the service so far as reliability, knowledge of duty, and energy" were concerned, and to kick them out for political reasons would "cause a very big stink" and "I do not want to have a hand in it. . . . I would rather resign" than "do the dirty work."

His father agreed but advised him from Vienna to try to manage it "without censure." Taft went to Washington to see President Arthur at the White House and made his feelings clear. The result was an announcement that Taft was resigning to resume the practice of law with his father's former partner, Harlan Lloyd, but that he would remain in office until March, 1883, to allow time for his successor to take over.

Relieved of the unhappy burdens of the revenue office, he regained his good disposition, and by the summer of 1883 was on his way to Europe for a vacation with his friend, Rufus Smith, to visit his mother and father in Vienna. They toured Ireland first, then Scotland and England, where they heard British statesman William Gladstone debate in the House of

Commons, and went on a walking trip through Switzerland before finally arriving in Vienna. By late October he was back in Cincinnati, to settle down at last to starting his career as a private attorney, handling his share of cases for the firm of Taft & Lloyd.

Although temporarily out of public office, he was still active in politics. The election of 1884 that nationally put Democrat Grover Cleveland in the White House turned to riot, brawls and wild disorder in Cincinnati and Taft was personally involved. He had been appointed chief election supervisor with a staff of sixty men as deputies to prevent fraud at the polls. But in many polling places there was free-for-all political warfare, with fist fights and even some shootings. As an aftermath, the House of Representatives sent a committee to Cincinnati to investigate and Taft was called as a witness. He testified that his deputies had done their best to prevent fraud and to halt intimidation of voters. Republicans congratulated him, Democrats denounced him, and all the investigation really proved was that it had been a dirty fight by the ward bosses on both sides.

But more than politics diverted Taft from the single-minded practice of law. He had been taking Nellie Herron out more frequently, to dinner, the theater, parties and dances, and they were both in an amateur theatrical group. Taft was the star of several plays and Nellie was his leading lady. In one comedy production he donned a costume skirt and a wig of flowing curls to portray an outsized Sleeping Beauty, which led the girls in the group to nickname him "Angel." He still dated other girls and Nellie went out with other young men. Taft explained in a letter to his mother that as much as he admired Nellie, she had so many other suitors that "I have not felt myself impelled to become one of them." And he showed his independence one week by taking Nellie to the theater on Monday and dating a different girl each night for the rest of the week.

Nellie, who had been teaching in a private school, was

making notes in her diary that confessed more interest in him than he realized or she would admit, and she found a way to bring him regularly to her home along with a group of other friends. She decided to establish a "salon," patterned after the fashionable literary gatherings of Europe, to be held every Saturday night so that her specially invited guests could engage in the "brilliant discussion of topics intellectual and economic," as she put it, "bent on improving our minds."

Taft, of course, was among those "specially invited," and in Nellie's company he showed an avid interest in the weekly pursuit of literature, philosophy and the writings of great men. The talk at the salon often turned to subjects more personal than intellectual and Nellie made the evenings pleasant by serving such snacks as broiled oysters or strawberries and cream. While she kept up the pretense of pursuing knowledge for its own sake, she wrote some lines to St. Valentine in her diary: "Now cheer him and cheer him still, for giving Will to Nellie, and giving Nellie to Will."

But if romance had come fully into his life, so had his old courtroom adversary, criminal lawyer Tom Campbell. For a time, all of Cincinnati was too aroused to think of much else. Fury against Campbell touched off rioting in which scores of men were killed or injured, and Taft soon became the crusading leader of a reform drive that, as Nellie later wrote, "became the history of our lives during that period."

** CHAPTER **

4

WILLIAM HOWARD TAFT might have remained a merely successful lawyer all his life if a Cincinnati horse dealer hadn't been murdered on Christmas Eve in 1883. The murder started a chain of events that Taft later said led "to all I have had since." What he meant, but modestly did not say, was that it created a situation that let him prove his ability.

For months, Cincinnati had been terrorized by a series of brutal crimes and a wave of robberies that had its frightened citizens demanding action. Emotions were inflamed by sensational newspaper reporting and by editorials warning that the "public safety" was threatened by a complete breakdown of law and order. Crime, it was said, was "running wild in the streets."

The county jail was called "a hotel for murderers" because it housed forty-two men accused of killings, along with others charged with various crimes, whose trials had been long delayed. Flaming editorials declared no resident of the city was safe as long as "criminals" escaped "just punishment." There were direct incitements for people to take the law into their own hands, with editorial thunder that "if the courts cannot enforce laws and protect society there is imminent danger that other ways will be sought and found." Much of the editorial fury centered upon lawyer Tom Campbell who was accused of working with corrupt politicians and criminal gangs to "thwart justice" as a "protector of crime."

On Christmas Eve, livery stable owner William Kirk, a boastful man who liked to flash big rolls of money, was clubbed, choked and robbed and his body was thrown into a ditch. Two of his stableboys, William Berner and Joseph Palmer, were caught spending some of his money in a saloon, and both confessed but each insisted the other had done the actual killing.

When Campbell became Berner's attorney at the trial in March, 1884, and despite the evidence, managed to get Berner off on a reduced charge of manslaughter instead of first-degree murder, public feeling turned to rage. The jury foreman was booed and hissed as he left the courtroom, jurors were threatened, and newspapers claimed "no honest jury" would have returned such a verdict.

On the night of March 28, an angry crowd gathered in Cincinnati's Music Hall for a protest meeting, in no mood to listen to pleas for moderation. There were open demands for a mass lynching and a mob of self-appointed avengers of justice started to move toward the county jail. When they began throwing bricks through the jail windows and battering at the gates, fire bells sounded a riot warning. Police held off the mob until state militia units arrived and the troops drove the people back. Unable to break into the jail, the crowd turned to the nearby courthouse, set it ablaze and burned it to the ground. Rioting and shooting went on into the next day and before the mass hysteria ended, forty-five people were dead and one hundred and twenty-five more had been injured.

Taft, like most other responsible citizens of Cincinnati, was sickened by what had happened. He had not been involved in the Berner trial and was dismayed by the mass meeting that had turned to riot. But he sincerely believed that Campbell and those associated with him were at the root of the evil that infected the court system. He decided an example should be made of Campbell, by legal means instead of mob emotion, to help restore public faith in the ability of the courts to enforce the law.

Within days after the riot, he presented a resolution to the Cincinnati bar association to amend the code of criminal procedure "to quicken the trial of cases and hasten the bringing of criminals to justice," and went with a committee to the state capital at Columbus with a proposed bill. He made speeches to civic clubs, calling for a reform of the county's judicial system to bring "faster and surer justice" by simplifying procedure and plugging loopholes in court administration.

Campbell was indicted on a charge of attempting to bribe one of the jurors in the Berner case, but escaped conviction when a hung jury failed to agree on a verdict. The lawyer who defended Campbell in the bribery trial was Joseph Foraker, soon to be Ohio's governor. Taft meanwhile had become an investigator for the bar association as it moved on its own in an attempt to throw Campbell out of the legal profession, on charges of misconduct as an attorney. Assigned to collect evidence that would be turned over to the bar's senior attorneys, he worked without pay, dug into every law case Campbell had ever been connected with, and spent the whole summer and fall traveling about Ohio to take statements and prepare thick files of evidence.

When the disbarment hearing against Campbell began in Cincinnati's District Court, in November, 1884, two other attorneys—both recognized leaders of the bar—were in charge of the prosecution. As junior counsel Taft's place was in the background, but on the day of final argument the senior attorney scheduled to sum up the charges against Campbell was kept home by illness and at the last minute Taft took his place. He emerged as the leading figure of the Campbell trial.

With all of Ohio excited by the case and every lawyer and politician interested, Taft addressed the court for more than four hours in an eloquent nonstop presentation that was careful in its logic and legal argument. But Campbell was a moving witness in his own behalf. Tears streaked his face as he pictured himself the victim of "wild public passion." There was ample proof that he had been involved in questionable practices, but he was absolved of all charges except a minor one and while the notoriety eventually did drive him out of practice in Cincinnati, he was not disbarred.

Taft lost his case, but won popular acclaim as a people's hero, a champion of "the forces of decency." His summation, even though it failed to convince the court, was highly praised by lawyers and judges. He had begun the Campbell hearing as an unimportant young attorney with a well-known name, who had gained some prominence by riding on his father's coattails; he came out of it a young man who had proven he could stand on his own, not merely as the politically favored son of the Honorable Alphonso Taft. He always felt that except for the opportunity of the Campbell trial and what followed, he might have remained a working partner in his father's old law firm for the rest of his life.

His friend, Rufus Smith, became county solicitor in January, 1885, and appointed Taft his assistant. He gained active experience trying civil cases and, more important to Taft, added $2,500 a year to his income, which he decided gave him enough to support a wife. He proposed to Nellie in April, but she kept him in doubt for a month and even then insisted their engagement be kept secret until she was certain.

All through the spring and summer he suffered the romantic torment of a lovesick young man desperately trying to convince her she had made the right decision. He sent her flowers, books of poetry, worried that she might change her mind, and became what his friends called "a mountain of misery." He wrote his father, who had been transferred from Vienna to St. Petersburg as American minister to Russia, that Nellie "persists in holding me in suspense."

When Nellie and her family went back East for a summer

vacation in New York's Adirondack Mountains, he could hardly bear it. Unable to stand the separation, he found an excuse to end it in one of her letters complaining about the lack of variety in the food offered at the resort where she was staying. He went to Cincinnati's fanciest grocery store, selected a box as big as a trunk, ordered it filled with every delicacy he could think of, and boarded a train and took it to her.

For two weeks, he stayed with Nellie and her family at the hotel in the Adirondacks, took her boating on the lake, walking in the woods, and read poetry aloud to her by the hour while she sat sketching pictures. They picnicked on the bank of a mountain stream and the fried potatoes Nellie cooked, "although they had fallen once or twice into the fire and been nearly destroyed," tasted to him "as fine as anything Delmonico could serve." Reaching for water lilies to give her while they were out rowing, he tipped the boat, but by the time his visit ended there was no doubt about their engagement and they made definite plans for a wedding the following June.

He returned to Cincinnati and plunged into political combat with Joseph Foraker, who was about to receive the Republican nomination for governor. With Hol Hollister, he went as a delegate to the party's state convention to oppose Foraker's nomination and was so disgusted, he wrote Nellie, that "it almost cured me of any desire to take part in politics." He had gotten into a brawl with a Foraker delegate who called him a liar. The man drew a pistol from his pocket and Taft slapped him across the face and disarmed him. "It was in a crowd in a narrow hall," he explained to Nellie, "and two or three persons interfered. . . ."

When he learned later that Foraker himself had made some remarks about him to a law clerk, Taft telephoned Foraker and dared him to repeat what he had said to his face. Foraker swore at him and accepted the challenge, but they never actually came to blows.

Nellie's return from the Adirondacks took Taft's mind off political warfare. They spent a good part of the winter before their marriage planning the house they meant to build on the lot her father had given them, overlooking the Ohio River in suburban Walnut Hills. The house cost $6,000 and Taft borrowed the money to finance the building. With his bachelor days about over, he was saving money for the first time and worrying some about his future financial responsibilities. Nellie already had become their financial manager, but when it came to making arrangements for their planned wedding trip to Europe she was less willing to trim the budget than he was.

She went to Washington for a brief visit in March, 1886, and had her wedding gown made while she was there. Taft sent her a somewhat prophetic note: "I hope you will think of me when you take your Sunday walk along the beautiful streets of Washington. I wonder, Nellie dear, if you and I will ever be there in any official capacity?" Then he added, in a joking reference to her money-managing instinct, "Oh, yes, I forgot; of course we shall, when you become Secretary of the Treasury."

Taft, as a friend put it, was a "jovial but nervous bridegroom," three times the size of his slender satin-gowned bride. The Episcopal ceremony was performed late in the afternoon of June 19, 1886, in the Herron home by the Reverend D. N. A. Hoge of Zanesville, who had married Nellie's parents. Taft's brother, Horace, was his best man and Nellie's bridesmaids were her sister, Maria, and Taft's sister, Fanny.

To save money, they had booked passage to England aboard the oldest and cheapest ship they could find, the *City of Chester,* which Nellie called a "slow old tub." Seasick the first few days, she was annoyed because nothing interfered with Taft's normally hearty appetite. But she enjoyed the lack of formality that let them dress in old clothes, and they soon were keeping a joint diary, one page for her and the opposite page for him, in which they made teasing comments about what each had written.

Most of their summer was spent in England and Scotland, Taft giving in to Nellie's desire to visit cathedrals, museums and literary sites, while she went with him to the old law courts of London. They had a good look at Queen Victoria in a royal procession, and made a quick trip to Paris, where Nellie went on a clothes-buying spree.

In Holland she bought some large delft plates, too big to go into their suitcase, and he toted them all over Europe in a wicker hand basket, complaining about them most of the way. The plates became a family joke. Safely brought across the Atlantic, they were smashed by the express company that shipped them to Cincinnati, so that Nellie finally was able to piece together only one plate. It was kept as a souvenir that Taft laughingly called "the memento of our first unpleasantness."

They began the year 1887 in their new house, but Taft had hardly settled down to practicing law again when he came home one evening, as Nellie told it, "looking so studiously unconcerned that I knew at once he had something to tell me." What he had to tell her was that he was about to be appointed a judge of the superior court. Nellie thought he was joking. "Don't try to be funny," she said. "That's perfectly impossible."

It had seemed as impossible to Taft. Superior court judges usually were elected, but Judge Judson Harmon wanted to retire and someone had to be appointed to fill his unexpired term. Harmon had been impressed by Taft's proposals for judicial reform and even more by his legal performance in the Campbell hearing. He strongly recommended Taft. Even so, Taft hardly expected to get it. At twenty-nine he was only seven years out of law school and there were men of far more experience and higher standing who were eager to become judges.

What seemed even more unlikely was that the appointment

would come to him from Governor Foraker, after their exchange of insults. Taft couldn't believe Foraker would be that generous. But Foraker surprised him. He issued a statement praising Taft for his "strong intellectual endowment" and "keen analytical mind" and welcomed Judge Harmon's suggestion that Taft would be the best man to succeed him.

Perhaps, as Nellie later said, Foraker came to have an opponent's admiration for Taft's ability in the Campbell case, "a lawyer's appreciation for a lawyer's efforts." But Foraker also had political reasons. Busy building a state Republican machine, with personal ambitions for the future, Foraker saw more to gain from Taft's support than from his enmity. Making Taft a judge would heal party rifts and please the voters who demanded reform. If Foraker could bury his personal feelings, so could Taft. Under the circumstances, he had every reason to be grateful.

He became a judge in March, 1887, and when his appointed term ran out, he stood for election to a full term of his own, campaigned actively, and was kept on the superior court by the voters. He won a three-to-two victory in the balloting. It was the only time in his life that he ever sought election to any public office until years later when he became President of the United States. He was appointed to all the other official positions he held.

✳✳ CHAPTER ✳✳

5

I LOVE judges and I love courts," Taft once said. "They are my ideals." When he took his place on the Ohio superior court it was for him what Nellie called "the welcome beginning of just the career he wanted."

But she wasn't as happy about it as he was. She was afraid he would lose his youthful enthusiasm and "more general contact with the world." Nellie had bigger ambitions for him and "began to fear the narrowing effects of the bench." Although she admitted he did not agree, she "dreaded to see him settled for good in the judiciary."

As a beginning judge, his opinions were generally cautious, conservative and wordy, but they did show his thoroughness and ability to penetrate complicated legal problems, and few of his decisions were upset by higher courts. He tried so hard to be impartial that attorneys who had been close friends sometimes complained he was stricter with them than with strangers.

His best remembered opinion as a superior court judge was in the case of *Moores & Co. vs. Bricklayers' Union.* When the contracting firm of Parker Brothers fired some union men, Cincinnati's bricklayers tried to cut off its supply of building materials by warning all suppliers not to sell to Parker.

Moores & Company, a dealer in lime used in bricklaying, ignored the union warning, sold lime to Parker, and had its products boycotted by the union. The bricklayers refused to work for any contractor in the city who had purchased supplies from Moores.

Moores & Company sued the union for loss of business, claiming the secondary boycott was a malicious conspiracy, and a jury awarded the company $2,500 damages. When the case came before the superior court on a union motion for a new trial, Taft and his two fellow judges ruled against the union. Some parts of his opinion were quite liberal for an age when many conservatives thought it should be against the law for workers to form unions at all. He held that it clearly was not against the law for workers to combine "to raise their wages or to obtain any mutual advantages," that every laborer had a right to "bestow his labor . . . according to his pleasure," and that "what one workman may do, many may do, and many may combine to do."

But when it came to the secondary boycott, he was firmly antiunion. By trying to use one company to hurt another, he ruled, the union had gone beyond the law. He held that by boycotting Moores' lime the union had tried to inflict "punishment and disaster," not to gain rightful benefits for workers but to show what would follow "a defiance of their demands." Such a boycott, he said, was both "malicious and illegal," and therefore the company was entitled to collect damages from the union and a new trial should be denied.

It was an opinion that was to be dragged out of the dusty court files years later when Taft was running for President. Quoted for him by some who claimed he had shown an early sympathy for organized labor, the opinion was quoted against him by others who charged he was among the first of the nation's judges to set a precedent that was a hard blow to unions when they were struggling for recognition. Taft never changed his mind. He remained against such labor boycotts and long afterwards cited his own *Moores* opinion in other cases he judged.

He took Nellie to Europe again the summer after he became a judge, but when they returned to Cincinnati he found his brother Peter dying of tuberculosis, and his father, who had ended his diplomatic missions, in extremely poor health and failing rapidly. Alphonso, suffering from lung and heart troubles, developed cardiac asthma, and went to San Diego, California, for rest and treatment.

There was happier family news when Nellie gave birth to their first child, an eight-pound boy, on September 8, 1889. When she first saw the expression on Taft's face afterwards, she laughed and told him not to look so conceited. He admitted in a note: "I have been accused of the unjudicial conduct of rushing out into the street after the boy came and yelling, 'Hurrah! For a man is born unto me!' " He wanted to name the baby Alphonso, after his father, but Nellie had chosen Robert, so they compromised and named their son Robert Alphonso Taft.

Nellie kept urging Taft toward greater ambitions, telling him he could be governor of Ohio if he would only try, but he laughed at such talk and was content to remain a superior court judge, hoping that someday in the long years ahead he might be considered for a place on the United States Supreme Court. Suddenly, that boyhood dream became an immediate, if unlikely, possibility.

There was a vacancy on the Supreme Court in 1889 and rumors were that President Benjamin Harrison would choose an Ohioan to fill it. Harrison had been born in Ohio, had gone to an Ohio college with Nellie's father, and had studied law in Cincinnati. Although at first it seemed somewhat ridiculous to Taft, he learned that some of his friends who were close to the President were working hard to win the Supreme Court appointment for him.

Among them was Judge Hiram Peck, who had been on the superior court when Taft first took his place on the bench.

Peck was joined by other jurists, lawyers and politicians in what Taft described to his father was "the innocent amusement of pushing me." He added that "I know the chance is only one in a million." But it was too great a chance to ignore. Taft and his friends soon were pulling every political wire within reach to influence President Harrison's decision. Former Yale classmates stirred up Republican support in New England, and Governor Joseph Foraker became Taft's chief advocate in Ohio.

President Harrison visited Cincinnati and Taft had himself named to the welcoming committee that boarded the Presidential train to make sure "the President had taken in who I was." Foraker talked to Harrison during the visit and gave Taft a "first-class recommendation." But Taft still considered "all this . . . very good fun and that is all," and wrote his father, "My chances of going to the moon and of donning a silk gown at the hands of President Harrison are about equal. I am quite sure if I were he I would not appoint a man of my age and position to that bench."

He read the President's mind well. Harrison decided that at thirty-two Taft was too young and that his judicial career was too new to place him on the Supreme Court. There were others who rated more serious consideration. But to Taft's complete surprise, the President did offer to make him the new Solicitor General of the United States.

Taft wasn't entirely sure he wanted it. He was happy as an Ohio judge, with a term that still had nearly three years to run, and if a place on the Supreme Court had been too much to expect, he still wanted to go on judging. However, Foraker strongly urged him to accept, and Nellie was even more eager. She was excited over the chance to go to Washington and by the fact that he would be associated with the nation's most important men. Nellie saw it as an escape for him from the narrow world of the courtroom and a way to the political career she wanted him to have. It was, as she later wrote, "exactly the kind of work I wished him to do." Finally, but still rather reluctantly, Taft resigned from the superior court to become the nation's solicitor general.

As solicitor general he would draft legal opinions for the President and members of the cabinet and would argue most of the government's cases before the Supreme Court. He wrote his father that he felt "entirely unfamiliar" with Federal law, and that he had "very little familiarity with the decisions of the Court." From California Alphonso answered that he was exceedingly proud of him and that his only advice was to "go ahead and fear not."

Taft arrived in Washington shortly after dawn on a cold February morning in 1890. He had been unable to sleep on the train, found nobody to greet him at the station, no porter to carry his heavy bag, and no restaurant open for breakfast. He trudged along to a hotel and then found his way to the Justice Department, where he had to introduce himself to Attorney General William Miller. After a hurried and unimpressive swearing-in ceremony was arranged, he went to inspect his new office, which bore "not the slightest resemblance" to his mental picture of what the solicitor general's office would be.

It was a single room, up three flights of stairs, with an old-fashioned and rather battered desk in one corner. When Taft asked about his staff he was told that if he wanted to dictate anything he could bellow down the hall and a telegrapher in the chief clerk's office would come to act as his stenographer when the telegraph wires were not too busy. His desk was piled with accumulated legal papers and Taft learned that among his other duties he would have to digest ten complicated cases he knew nothing about, prepare briefs, and argue them before the Supreme Court adjourned in June. He wrote Nellie that he felt "dismally unimportant" and was utterly discouraged by the "very disheartening outlook."

But within a few days he was meeting people, being invited out to dinners, and had decided that Washington after all might be a city "as friendly as Cincinnati." Two weeks later, when Nellie arrived with baby Bobby, the new solicitor general felt far less an unknown man. He had met President Harrison, who invited him to the White House, and as he wrote his father, "I am gradually getting acquainted with the prominent people here and I have no doubt that . . . I shall have a pretty general knowledge of the persons who run things."

He and Nellie rented a small house on DuPont Circle, where he converted a second-floor room into a law library, but Nellie was annoyed when he added thirty volumes of English chancery reports, which she considered extravagant. She thought he was still too preoccupied with law, and she found it hard to interest him in the social events of Washington society. They did attend occasional receptions and diplomatic parties, but most of their evenings were spent in the company of law officials, attorneys, Supreme Court Justices, and their wives.

Washington's oppressive summer heat and his own physical heaviness troubled Taft, and when doctors warned that his weight might affect his heart he seriously tried to reduce. "Nothing will do for me but regular and hearty exercise," he wrote Nellie, who had taken Bobby with her to vacation at the cooler Massachusetts seashore. "You must make yourself a thorn in my side to that end, darling." He bought a horse to take daily rides for exercise and he began the battle against increasing fat that he would fight all his life.

He was not happy at his work and at times felt there was much more than he could do. But his association with the President, cabinet members and leaders and Congress was giving him a thorough if sometimes disillusioning inside knowledge of the high-level operations of national government. He had been on the job only a few months when Attorney General Miller became ill and he temporarily had to take full charge of the Justice Department as acting Attorney General. "What with appointments, dilatory officials throughout the country, and cranks," he wrote, "one's time is all occupied and nothing is accomplished."

President Harrison became an example to him of the way a President should not deal with members of Congress. Publicly, Harrison was an eloquent speaker, but in his personal dealings he was almost completely lacking in charm and candor. Taft was not the only one who found his frigid reserve and extreme dignity somewhat chilling. "The President is not popular with members of either house," Taft informed his father. "His manner of treating them is not at all fortunate, and when they have an interview with him they generally come away mad."

But one friend of those years Taft did find he could talk to frankly was Theodore Roosevelt. A year younger than Taft, Roosevelt had served in the New York legislature and had been an unsuccessful candidate for mayor of New York City before coming into Harrison's administration as Civil Service Commissioner, where his vigorous crusading for reforms troubled some of the old guard Republicans who had helped bring him to Washington.

By nature, Taft and Roosevelt were opposites: Roosevelt was bold, impulsive, restless with energy, often impatient with the slow workings of government and technicalities of law; Taft was calm, judicial, easygoing and unhurried, with a deep respect for the exact letter of the law and for working within formalities. Each in his own way, they got things accomplished, and they took a liking to each other that began what was to be the most important friendship in Taft's life.

Taft was not only getting a valuable education in the workings of government and the whole Federal court system, but also a thorough grounding in the practice of constitutional law and in Supreme Court procedure. Despite what he admitted were his unimpressive first attempts to argue cases before the Supreme Court, he became very successful in winning court decisions for the government.

He went home from the Court "a great deal discouraged"

after arguing his first case in April, 1890, and wrote his Ohio friend, Judge Peck, that "I do not think I acquitted myself with credit. . . . I do not find myself at all easy or fluent on my feet. I am afraid I never shall be." Still somewhat discouraged after his second appearance at the Court, Taft nevertheless regained his good humor and was able to poke fun at himself in a letter to his father. He jokingly described the justices as "a lot of mummies" and wrote that "they seem to think when I begin to talk that it is a good chance to read all the letters that have been waiting for some time, to eat lunch, and to devote their attention to correcting proof, and other matters that have been delayed until my speech."

But during his first year as solicitor general, he won fifteen of the eighteen cases he argued before the Court. The case that drew the most attention involved a dispute between Britain and the United States over seal hunting in the Bering Sea that had feelings in both countries at the boiling point. American revenue cutters, to protect the great Pribilof Islands seal herd from slaughter, had been ranging over the sea as far as sixty miles from shore chasing down the vessels of invading seal hunters, many of which were British-Canadian and the British government had protested. Congress had called on President Harrison to close the Bering Sea to foreign seal hunters and to use force if necessary to keep them out.

While attempts were underway to arbitrate the dispute, a Canadian schooner was seized by a revenue cutter and ordered condemned and forfeited by a Federal court at Sitka, Alaska. The British government appealed to the Supreme court for a writ to prohibit the sale of the vessel, in effect asking the Court to decide that the President, the State Deparment, and Congress were backing illegal actions.

Taft spent many nights as well as days preparing a three hundred page brief that amounted to a history of seal hunting from the time the Russians first came to Alaska. He argued that Britain had no right to ask the Court to review a question of international dispute at the same time it was actively negotiating that dispute with other branches of the government. He won his case and high praise from prominent lawyers. The Supreme Court agreed with him, upheld the lower Federal court ruling, refused to halt the sale of the captured sealing vessel, and sent Britain back to the negotiating table.

But despite the satisfaction he gained from "putting a flea in the ear of the British government," and from other Supreme Court victories, Taft was still unhappy in Washington. He longed to get away from the center of national politics and to return to a courtroom where he could be a judge.

** CHAPTER **

6

TAFT resigned as Solicitor General of the United States in March, 1892, to become United States Circuit Judge for the Sixth Judicial Circuit, with headquarters in Cincinnati but jurisdiction over all of Kentucky, Michigan and Tennessee as well as Ohio. He had been campaigning for the position for a year, since Congress had passed a law calling for the appointment of new judges and creating Circuit Courts of Appeal.

"Federal judgeships like that don't lie around loose, and if you don't get them when you can you will not get them when you would," he said when he decided to go after the appointment in the spring of 1891. Nellie was against it and did all she could to change his mind. The thought of his leaving the center of political power to return to the bench dismayed her. She feared he would be "fixed in a groove for the rest of his life" and warned him, "If you get your heart's desire, my darling, it will put an end to all the opportunities you now have of being thrown with the bigwigs."

Judging was Taft's "heart's desire." He knew what he wanted and went after it, against Nellie's pleading. Discreetly, he pulled political wires again to get President Harrison to appoint him. Senators and Representatives used their influence, prominent lawyers telegraphed Harrison, and the Ohio bar association recommended Taft as a man who had "proved his ability in judicial service." But it still took months before the President made up his mind.

Taft dropped everything else to hurry across the country early in May, 1891, when word came from California that his father was dying. During the last days, Alphonso was unconscious most of the time. In the final hours, as Taft sat at his bedside, there was a moment when his father's mind cleared, and as Taft wrote Nellie, "he looked up at me in the sweetest way imaginable and said to me, 'Will, I love you beyond expression.' "

Alphonso Taft died on May 21, at the age of eighty-one, and Taft wrote that "Father has been a kind of guardian angel to me in that his wishes for my success have been so strong and intense as to bring it . . ." One of his father's last wishes had been that he would get the appointment as circuit judge. When President Harrison finally named him to the new position, Taft's only disappointment was that has father hadn't lived long enough to share his pride in it.

Taft wore a new silk robe he had bought for the occasion when he took his place on the circuit bench in Cincinnati, where he would preside over both civil and criminal trials. As a judge of the Circuit Court of Appeals he also traveled the circuit to such cities as Cleveland, Toledo, Detroit and Nashville.

Nellie, although far from resigned to her fate, had accepted his decision that again made her a judge's wife. She returned to Cincinnati ahead of him to find them a place to live since their old home in Walnut Hills had been leased to tenants. To her complaint that his low judge's salary of only $6,000 a year would make paying the household bills a "close squeeze," Taft replied, "I don't see that people with very modest incomes don't live as happily as those that have fortunes."

Their concern over finances didn't keep them from going to Canada for a vacation in the summer of 1892, at Murray

Bay on the St. Lawrence River, a spot which was to become their favorite vacation place in the years that followed. He also fully enjoyed the social life connected with his circuit travels, and took pleasure in attending dinners, making speeches and winning new friends. But it was the courtroom that gave Taft real satisfaction and a sense of accomplishment.

During his years as a circuit judge he wrote two hundred and sixty opinions, twenty of them within a single session of two months. He gained a national reputation for contributing substantially to judicial thought, for scholarship in law journal writings, and for programs of court reform. Some of his decisions in labor and antitrust cases set precedents cited by other courts, including the Supreme Court. He also gained the political admiration of conservatives, and the lasting hatred of organized labor.

His first important labor decision grew out of a strike of engineers against the Toledo, Ann Arbor and North Michigan Railway. When the railroad refused to arbitrate demands for higher pay, the national Brotherhood of Locomotive Engineers notified its men on eleven rail systems in Ohio and neighboring states not to handle freight to or from the connecting Toledo and Ann Arbor line. The struck railroad sought court action, claiming the union had no right to use the other non-striking railroads to enforce its wage demands. Taft agreed that the union was attempting an illegal secondary boycott, and issued an injunction on April 3, 1893, to restrain the Brotherhood of Locomotive Engineers from putting the union freight ban into effect on the rail lines feeding shipments to the Toledo and Ann Arbor.

Another of Taft's opinions that soon made labor hate him more was an outgrowth of the violent Pullman strike in Chicago that became a landmark in the long struggle for union recognition. Eugene Debs and his pioneer American Railway Union declared a boycott against moving any Pullman car over any railroad in the United States. With the nation's railroad traffic paralyzed, President Grover Cleveland sent an

Army regiment into Chicago to break the strike and move the mails, resulting in pitched battles between soldiers and strikers, destruction, rioting, bloodshed and the deaths of twelve men.

One of Debs' lieutenants, Frank Phelan, meanwhile had come to Cincinnati to lead Ohio's railroad workers in supporting the Pullman boycott, which threatened a tie-up of all rail lines into Cincinnati. As circuit judge, Taft was directly concerned because the Cincinnati Southern Railroad, which had gone into receivership, was under the jurisdiction of the Federal court. He spent his nights sleeping in the customs house "with a force of fifty deputy marshals on one side of the river and seventy-five on the other" to keep order, and found himself "conducting a kind of police court" as men were "constantly being arrested" and brought before him.

Taft issued an injunction to restrain Phelan from "inciting, encouraging, ordering or in any other manner causing the employees of the receiver . . . to obstruct the operation" of the Cincinnati Southern. Phelan was put under bond, but soon was arrested on a charge of ignoring the injunction in contempt of court. He denied the charge, a trial was set, and a week was spent hearing testimony in a courtroom jammed wtih spectators. Businessmen were angry and uneasy. Some Cincinnatians feared riots like those in Chicago and others were outraged by delays in freight and mail deliveries. But to the union men, hot with a sense of injustice, Phelan's trial was a persecution of labor.

On July 13, 1894, Taft handed down his decision *In Re Phelan,* with a carefully written opinion that took him more than an hour to read. In it, he spelled out in terms that were in advance of most of the legal thinking of his time what was one of the first clear judicial statements from a high Federal court in defense of labor's legitimate right to organize and to strike.

"It is of benefit to them and to the public that laborers should unite in their common interest and for lawful pur-

poses," he said. "They have labor to sell. If they stand together, they are often able, all of them, to command better
prices for their labor than when dealing singly with rich
employers . . ." They also had a right to raise funds, and a
right to appoint officers to advise them "in their relations with
their employer," Taft went on. "They may unite with other
unions. The officers they appoint, or any other person to
whom they choose to listen, may advise them peaceably to
leave the employ of their employer because any of the terms
of their employment are unsatisfactory."

Phelan, if he had come to Cincinnati to urge and carry out
a legitimate strike, "would not have been liable to contempt
even if the strike much impeded the operation of the road
under order of the court," Taft said. "His action in giving the
advice, or in issuing an order based on unsatisfactory terms
of employment, would have been entirely lawful."

But instead, in Taft's opinion, Phelan had come to carry out
an illegal boycott, a purpose "unlawful by the law of Ohio
and the laws of the United States," and he had, in contempt
of the court injunction, incited workers to quit their jobs. To
punish a man for contempt, Taft said, was "the most dis-
agreeable duty a court has to perform, but . . . if the orders
of the court are not obeyed, the next step is into anarchy . . ."
He found Phelan "guilty as charged" and sent him to prison
for six months.

Taft was bitterly denounced by labor leaders and liberals
for sending Phelan to jail, as he knew he would be. In several
other cases his opinions permanently benefited labor with
decisions that set precedents in workmen's compensation and
safety laws, but they did little to cool the furor over his anti-
labor injunctions and the jailing of Debs' lieutenant. Yet
some of his decisions in other areas were against big business.
Taft took a firm early stand against trusts and monopolies.
Among the more important of his opinions as a circuit judge
was his antitrust ruling in what came to be known as the
Addystone Pipe Case.

Congress in 1890, to meet increasing demands for control of corporations, had passed the Sherman Antitrust Law, declaring illegal any combination or contract in restraint of trade among the states, but attempts to enforce it were blocked by court decisions, including one by the Supreme Court, and for a time the law was almost dead. Taft's ruling helped strengthen the Sherman Antitrust Law, so that it survived with revived interest into the years when it became a more effective weapon against monopolies.

The Addystone Pipe and Steel Company of Cincinnati was accused by the Federal government of joining with other iron pipe companies in the Ohio and Mississippi valleys to block competition by fixing prices and sharing profits. When a lower Federal court dismissed the suit, the government appealed to the circuit court. The companies argued that their agreement was valid under common law and that they had no monopoly that could control prices because their total sales amounted to less than thirty per cent of the nation's production of iron pipe.

Taft, in his opinion for the circuit court, went back to the fundamentals of English common law to show that it offered no protection against applying the Sherman Antitrust Act to a monopoly. He held that Addystone and the other companies did have power to control prices, that they were "able to deprive the public in a large territory of the advantages otherwise accruing to them" from nearby factories, and that by secret agreements and rigged bids on contracts they forced the public to pay more than it should for iron pipe.

He declared that it was "a direct restraint upon interstate commerce" and was "on its face an extensive scheme to control the whole commerce among thirty-six states in cast-iron pipe." Upholding the government's case against the companies, he entered a decree "perpetually enjoining the defendants" from continuing the combination or doing any business under it.

His interests in judicial reform and in raising the standards of legal education led him in 1896 to take on the extra work of being dean of his legal alma mater, the Cincinnati Law School, and also of teaching two classes a week in real property law. He helped unite the school with the University of Cincinnati and introduced the case system of law study. For the next four years, in addition to his full-time duties as a circuit judge, he was administrator of the law school and a teacher, although he later joked, "As a teacher I had a hard time trying to keep ahead of the class."

But he wasn't interested when some of the members of the Yale Corporation suggested that he give up his place on the circuit court to become president of Yale University, as successor to Timothy Dwight who had resigned. There were, Taft answered, "insuperable objections to my accepting." Although he didn't say so, his reasons included a renewed hope that he soon might have a place on the Supreme Court.

His stature as a judge had grown so it seemed almost certain that he eventually would be appointed. When Associate Justice Howell Jackson died in 1895, Taft was prominently mentioned as his possible replacement. He hurried to Washington for a quick sounding out of the possibilities, had a twenty-minute talk with President Cleveland, and reported to Nellie that "almost every person I met spoke of my coming as a certainty."

Taft's hope that Democrat Cleveland might put him on the Court soon faded, but after the election he was even more optimistic that the appointment would come from the new Republican President, William McKinley. He was content meanwhile to remain a circuit judge and to wait. Life in Cincinnati was pleasant and there was added family happiness in the fact that he and Nellie were about to have their third and last child, Charles Taft II, who was to be born September 20, 1897.

** CHAPTER **

7

JUDGE TAFT was dictating an opinion in his circuit court chambers in Cincinnati one January day in 1900 when a boy knocked on the door and handed him a telegram that read: "I would like to see you in Washington on important business within the next few days." It was from President McKinley, and although Taft had no idea what the President wanted, he hoped it meant that at last he was about to be appointed to the Supreme Court.

His relations with McKinley had been close. It was through Taft's suggestion that his old Yale classmate, John Porter, had become the President's private secretary. Taft's influence with McKinley had also helped another friend, Theodore Roosevelt, become Assistant Secretary of the Navy, although Taft hadn't been alone in supporting Roosevelt for the job.

All the way to Washington, Taft thought about the Supreme Court appointment. There was no vacancy on the Court, but he decided perhaps McKinley had been informed that one of the justices was about to retire. When he reached the White House, he found the President and several members of the cabinet waiting for him. But what the President said completely floored him.

"Judge, I would like to have you go to the Philippines,"

McKinley told him. "We must establish a government out there and I would like you to help me do it."

When Taft recovered from his shock, he told the President he was sorry, but he would have to refuse. "I am not in sympathy with your policy, Mr. President," he said. "I am sorry you have got the Philippines. I don't want them and I think you ought to have a man who is in sympathy with taking them over."

According to the story Taft later told of the interview, McKinley answered, "Well, you don't want them any less than I do, but we have got them, and I think in dealing with them I can trust a man who did not want them in the beginning better than I can a man that did."

Taft had been out of sympathy with the Spanish-American War, which he considered an "unnecessary war," especially after it became not a crusade to free the Cubans from Spanish oppression but an imperialistic war of Far Eastern conquest. Once the war started, he had patriotically supported it, but he still took a dim view of the flag-waving demands that it was America's "manifest destiny" to become a world power. Unlike Theodore Roosevelt, who had been the most furious warmonger in Washington, calling President McKinley everything but a traitor for not getting into the war fast enough, Taft had shared none of the thirsting desire for personal combat that had led Roosevelt to glory as the heroic Rough Rider of San Juan Hill.

After much soul-searching, Taft had managed to convince himself that it had been impossible for McKinley to withstand the overwhelming demand of the American people for war with Spain. But he had strongly opposed taking the Philippines as "a far stretch of the controlling hand" and had been in favor of giving the Filipinos full independence. Yet the Philippines had been taken, and America apparently meant to stay, so Taft felt "now that we were there, we were under the most sacred duty to give them a good form of government."

A fact-finding commission, headed by Cornell University's president, Jacob Schurman, had returned from the Philippines with a lengthy report. McKinley explained that he wanted Taft to head a new commission to construct a civil government, which would replace American military rule against which the Filipinos were in revolt. It would be only a temporary assignment, the President said, one that probably wouldn't take more than a few months.

Taft disagreed. He thought the building of a government in the Philippines might take years and he wanted no part of it. He had no training for such a task, there were others better suited for it, and he much preferred to remain a judge. He had come to Washington with the hope of becoming a Supreme Court Justice and suddenly was being asked "to go ten thousand miles away from home," to sacrifice his place on the circuit court, and perhaps his entire judicial career.

The President reassured him about that. McKinley promised, according to Taft, "that if you give up this judicial office at my request you shall not suffer. If I last, and the opportunity comes, I shall appoint you." McKinley even hinted that if the vacancy came he would make him Chief Justice. "If I am here," the President told him, "you will be here."

Secretary of War Elihu Root, in charge of Philippine affairs and a friend Taft had known since his days in Washington as Solicitor General, was called in to help convince him. Root argued that Taft had to accept, that it was his "duty to the country" when it was "confronted with one of the gravest problems in its history." Framing a Philippine government, Root said, was essentially a lawyer's job, one Taft could do well, one that would make him "a broader, better judge" if he were later called to the Supreme Court. President McKinley also stressed "the duty of an American called upon to serve, to do so at any cost."

Taft asked the President for a week to make up his mind, but after being talked to by McKinley and Root, he had "a feeling when I went out of that room" that if Nellie agreed "I would probably go to the Philippines." He arrived home in Cincinnati three days later with "an expression so grave," as Nellie put it, "that I thought he must be facing impeachment."

But she was overjoyed and eagerly urged him to accept. Whatever additional convincing he needed, Nellie supplied. Taft said later, "I was thrown into the Philippines against my will—I won't say that, for I am a person I presume who could say yes or no—but I mean I was led into it." He finally sent McKinley his acceptance and resigned as judge of the Sixth Circuit Court, which Nellie said was "the hardest thing he ever did."

While Nellie made "happy preparations" for their adventure, Taft went back to Washington for detailed instructions and to discuss the appointment of the four other men who would serve with him on the Philippine Commission. "In less than two months," he wrote, "I found myself, my wife and three children . . . on the way across the Pacific to become responsible . . . for the government of eight million people whose very existence I had only become dimly conscious of in the two years previous."

What he knew about the Philippines was about what the average American knew, which was practically nothing. America had taken the islands under the peace treaty with Spain for a payment of twenty million dollars, rather than leave them under Spanish rule, or let them be captured by some other nation or fall into anarchy, and Americans had moved in to stay, to establish power in the far Pacific and to expand trade with the Orient. In fighting worse than any against Spain, American troops had killed thousands of Filipinos to "pacify" them.

Rebel leader Emilio Aguinaldo, who had led the Filipino uprising against Spanish rule in the belief that the conquering Americans would give his people freedom, and who had set up a rebel republic, had also led the now dying rebellion against the Americans when it seemed that the United States meant to establish a colonial military rule just as harsh as that of the Spaniards. American military command had been in supreme power and civil government had ceased to exist.

But America's new policy of control was to be different from that imposed upon colonies by most world powers. The official instructions to the commission, signed by President McKinley after Secretary of War Root had written them with Taft's help, called for the Filipinos to be given the greatest possible voice in their own affairs, so as to lead them gradually toward self-government. All the protections of the American Bill of Rights, except trial by jury and the right to bear arms, were to be granted. No person was to be "deprived of life, liberty or property without due process of law," either by the new civil commissioners or by the military command.

The Filipinos were not to get immediate independence, but they were to get the promise of it in time. Taft was greatly responsible for writing into the President's instructions the pledge that the new government was to be "designed not for our satisfaction, or for the expression of our theoretical views, but for the happiness, peace and prosperity of the people of the Philippine Islands, and the measures adopted should be made to conform to their customs, their habits, and even to their prejudices, to the fullest extent consistent with the ac-complishment of . . . just and effective government."

He and his fellow commissioners would have several months after reaching the islands to study, plan and hold public hearings. On September 1, 1900, the commission would be clothed with the full legislative powers that had been held by the military governor, and would have the task of building from scratch a whole new system of government for millions of people who had enjoyed little voice in governing them-selves under centuries of Spanish rule or in the more recent years of American occupation.

The commissioners would control appropriations and would be in charge of civil government, but the plan was for the Army commander to remain in charge of Army operations, and also for him to remain chief executive as Military Governor of the Philippines. The President called for the "most perfect cooperation" between the military and civil branches, with the Secretary of War to act as final authority.

To the tooting of harbor whistles and the cheers of a handkerchief-waving dockside crowd, Taft and his commissioners and their families sailed from San Francisco aboard the U.S. Army transport *Hancock* on April 17, 1900. The Golden Gate was hardly out of sight when he called the men into the ship's conference room to begin the commission's first regular meeting.

He kept them at work most of the voyage, but there was also time for sightseeing at stops along the way. Taft enjoyed surf riding in a native canoe at Honolulu and met the Emperor of Japan at an imperial reception in Tokyo. Nellie, her sister, Maria, and the Taft children remained temporarily in Yokohama while Taft went on to the Philippines.

** CHAPTER **

8

THERE was no dockside crowd to greet Taft when the *Hancock* reached Manila on the hot Sunday morning of June 3, 1900. Among the natives, subjected to stern control by the occupying American Army, there was little hope that the coming of still another group of Americans would bring them freedom from harsh restrictions. And the military governor, General Arthur MacArthur, had no desire whatever to welcome Taft and his commission to the Philippines. The general pointedly ignored them, except for sending an aide who informed them that he would be willing to receive them at his office the following day.

When Taft and the commissioners went ashore on Monday, there "was not a Filipino in sight" as they were taken in a carriage between two files of soldiers to government headquarters. Taft had been sweating in the sun but said that when he entered MacArthur's office the general's manner was so frigid it stopped his perspiration. After a handshake that "dripped icicles," MacArthur informed Taft "that he regarded our coming as a personal reflection on him and that while he was, of course, obliged to submit to our presence there, he resented it nevertheless." The general resented being asked to share any part of what had been his supreme command

and bluntly told the commissioners he saw no reason for civilians to "intrude" upon military operations in the Philippines. The only way to enforce civilization upon the Islands, he said, was by gun and bayonet and the Filipinos would need "bayonet treatment" for at least a decade.

MacArthur assigned the commissioners an office of one small room they could hardly walk around in "without climbing over desks and chairs." Taft also was discouraged when he first saw the house the Army had arranged for him to rent in suburban Malate. In bad repair, it needed plumbing, had holes in the floors and a garden overgrown with weeds, with a yard worn bare from having been used to pasture Army horses. But he decided to make the best of it and in time, it became a home he loved. Right on Manila Bay, it had a broad back porch where whatever breeze there was brought some relief from the oppressive heat.

He was warned that no man could work as hard in the Philippine climate as he did back in the States, but he ignored the warning and set himself a twelve-hour work day. When the commission's public hearings to determine conditions began, most Filipinos were hostile and reluctant to testify, fearing the commission would treat them no better than the Army had. But when they learned that the commission was hated by the Army, the people seemed more willing to cooperate. The natives decided that if the Army was against the commission, then the commission must be on their side.

Even more important to Taft's success in the islands was his understanding of the pride of the Filipinos and their resentment against any implication that they were inferior human beings. He had been disheartened to discover that many Army men and their wives regarded "the Filipino ladies and men as 'niggers' and not fit to be associated with," and he declared, "we propose, so far as we are able, to banish this idea." He wrote Nellie that when she came to join him "one of the things we have to do here is to extend hospitality to Filipino families" because the "Army circles definitely and distinctly decline to have anything to do with them. . . . I need your assistance in taking a different course."

Taft welcomed Filipinos to his home, joined in their parties and festivities, respected and encouraged their native customs and traditions. His letters to Washington were filled with recommendations for better understanding. He insisted that the color line was never to be drawn at any official or unofficial affair in which he took part. Taft came to admire the Filipinos and to have a real fondness for those he publicly called his "brown brothers."

But Army men mocked Taft's phrase about "brown brothers" in a song popular among soldiers in the Philippines. Still bushwhacking their way through jungles and mountains to wipe out remaining pockets of resistance and to put fear into the hearts of any natives who might be tempted to sympathize with Aguinaldo's rebels, they sang a rousing chorus of Army hatred against the Filipino, which ended:

> *"He may be a brother of William H. Taft,*
> *But he ain't no friend of mine!"*

Taft repeatedly complained to Secretary Root about the Army attitude, not only on humanitarian grounds, but because it made his task of civil government more difficult. He said some soldiers were boasting that the United States meant to turn the Filipinos into slaves who would be hitched to carriages in place of horses, and were spreading rumors of imprisonment and cruel torture that provided propaganda for rebel agents to stiffen resistance.

Aside from planning and taking preliminary steps, there was not much the commission could do until after the Presidential election of 1900 back in the United States. If McKinley were defeated for reelection, Taft felt that the commission's labors in the Philippines would be in vain. Theodore Roosevelt, who had become McKinley's somewhat reluctant running mate, wrote his friend Taft in August that he would rather have been Taft's assistant in the Philippines than Vice President. But in November the good news came from home that McKinley and Roosevelt had been overwhelmingly elected and Taft and the commission actively began to put their program into effect.

The antiquated Spanish system of government, broken down by insurrection and replaced by martial law, was not much of a framework to build upon. Taft's new government had to adopt measures to fit the needs of an archipelago of eleven large islands and thousands of smaller ones, inhabited by a multiracial population of Malayan, Polynesian, Spanish and Asiatic backgrounds, educated city-dwellers and primitive tribesmen, who spoke innumerable dialects and shared no common language. He issued a proclamation setting forth the powers of the commission and announced that it would welcome criticism and suggestions and that no legislation would be adopted without advance public hearings, some of which lasted for months. Gradually he and the commissioners began drawing up laws for city and regional governments, courts, schools, public works, taxes and a hundred other needs.

Taft's first concern was to end the political spoils system that had operated under Spanish rule to fill "useless offices with favorites." He drafted a law to put every employee of the new government under civil service, with promotion to be based on competitive examinations. When he turned to the court system, Taft found that the whole body of Philippine law had become tangled and confused by conflicting regulations that followed rebellion and American occupation. He drew up new codes to revise both civil and criminal law and court procedure. A new Judiciary Act, adopted after eight months of hearings, established fourteen districts, to put courts within easy access of the people, provided for justices of peace as well as higher courts, and created a Supreme Court with a Filipino as Chief Justice.

Taft and the commission ordered old schools reopened, new ones built, and a Department of Public Instruction was established. Six hundred young college men and women were brought from the United States to staff the schools as the first of many American "blackboard pioneers." Free schooling for all, Taft declared, must be available everywhere in the islands. The schools were soon crowded and their popularity helped win the friendship of Philippine villagers as much as anything else the new government did.

The commission's major task was the establishment of municipal and provincial governments "in which the natives of the islands, both in the cities and in rural areas, shall be afforded the opportunity to manage their own affairs . . . subject to the least degree of supervision." Filipinos were to be chosen for top offices and councils would be elected by the people, although the commission retained controls.

Taft decided it was vital to visit the places where the first town governments were started so that he and the other commissioners personally could explain the new system to the people. His first trip was to a number of cities and villages on Luzon. Later in the spring of 1901 he and the commissioners and their families, along with a party that included sixty newspaper correspondents, boarded the Army transport *Sumner* for a much longer journey to eighteen distant southern provinces of the Philippines. Welcomed by native leaders and tribal chieftains, Taft made speeches, and attended fiestas, banquets and cockfights staged for his entertainment.

"I had to learn the stately Spanish quadrille called the *rigodón,* with which every properly conducted ball was opened," he wrote. "It was my business to lead out the wife of the mayor, or the governor of the province." The Filipino women usually were small and dainty and the contrast with Taft's enormous bulk as they danced together set Americans who were present to laughing, but "never disturbed the solemnity of the Filipinos," as he put it. They treated the dignified formality of the dance "almost as if it had been a religious ceremony."

Within months after the commission began passing its laws,

Taft was able to report that many local and regional governments had been established. The civil service system had been started and natives were being appointed to positions, schools had been increased, new courts were in operation, and tax and currency revisions were in effect. Harbor improvements as well as the building of badly needed roads and other public works were underway, and nearly all important rebel leaders except Aguinaldo had surrendered.

Aguinaldo had escaped every trap set for him as thousands of soldiers searched over the islands, but in March, 1901, it was learned that he was hiding somewhere in the mountains of northern Luzon, his forces dwindled and food and ammunition low. American General Frederick Funston led a surprise raid on the rebel camp and captured him. He was brought to Manila, still a hero to Filipinos. Taft refused demands to deport him to Guam and saw to it that no inflammatory official statements were issued against him. Aguinaldo was treated as an honored prisoner of war, and on April 19, 1901, he finally took the oath of allegiance to the United States and was granted freedom. The insurrection feebly flickered on in remote places, but the life had gone out of it.

Taft believed the time had come to put an end to the remaining authority of the military governor. For months he had been pointing out in reports to Washington that the major flaw in the commission's structure was in allowing the Army commander to remain chief executive. Secretary Root and President McKinley agreed. They told Taft that an act was being put through Congress to bring about the change. The President also decided that since Taft had done such an outstanding job as head of the commission he should be America's first civil governor of the Philippines.

** CHAPTER **

9

THOUSANDS of Filipinos crowded Manila's Cathedral Plaza on the Fourth of July, 1901, for the inauguration of their first civil governor. With a blare of trumpets and a roll of drums, Taft appeared, the band played and the crowd cheered. Beside him walked General MacArthur, about to retire as military governor, and General Adna Chaffee, who was to replace MacArthur as head of military operations. Taft delivered a simple inaugural address and afterwards moved into Malacanan Palace, traditional dwelling place of the rulers of the Philippines.

The palace looked like an over-built summer hotel and like such hotels was well supplied with swarms of mosquitoes. There was much entertaining to do, and although his salary as governor was $20,000 a year palace living was so expensive Taft wrote Secretary Root, "I do not expect to have a cent left." When he learned that electricity for one month cost $306 he worriedly went around turning off some of the palace lights to economize.

As governor, he remained head of the Philippine commission, which was to be a governing board for the islands. To give the people a greater voice, three Filipino commissioners were added to serve equally under Governor Taft

with the American commissioners. He had wanted five Filipinos added and had even considered naming former rebel
leader Aguinaldo as one of them, but those suggestions had
been overruled as too liberal. Taft set up new government
departments, appointed commissioners to head them, and
pushed forward new legislation. He overcame Army objections to trusting natives with weapons and passed an act to
arm, drill and equip a constabulary force to provide the
populace with police protection by Filipinos. A Board of
Health was created to plan better medical and sanitation
facilities, and he reorganized postal services, and began a
long-running battle with Congress to lower duties and improve
Philippine trade.

He also found it necessary to make more trips into the
interior. The climate, anxieties and overwork seriously
affected his health. Almost overcome by the heat during a
two-week trip in August into the remote mountains of Luzon,
he was nearly drowned on the way back when a native boat
in which he was riding was capsized by the surf. He had
returned to his Manila office on the morning of what was
September 7 in the Philippines when he received an urgent
cablegram from Washington that left him in such a state of
shock he failed to appear for lunch at Malacanan Palace.
When he finally arrived, as his guests were about to leave,
he still seemed stunned, and Nellie hurried across the dining
room to ask what was wrong. Taft said, "The President has
been shot."

President McKinley, shaking hands with well-wishers at
the Pan-American Exposition in Buffalo, had been fatally
wounded by anarchist Leon Czolgosz. Eight nights later he
died and Theodore Roosevelt, who had been "shelved" in the
Vice Presidency to put him politically out of the way, became
the new President of the United States. He was Taft's friend,
but a new administration meant upheavals, and Taft had
lost a strong and certain ally in McKinley.

In the Philippines, the assassination brought serious unrest.

There were fresh demands for immediate Philippine independence, countered by renewed cries from the militarists that
the Army should be put back in full control. After months
of comparative quiet, the remnants of rebel bands began
making guerrilla attacks on remote outposts. Late in September an Army infantry company in the village of Balangiga,
on Samar Island, was ambushed in a surprise attack by a
rebel band that swarmed out of the hills while the soldiers
were having breakfast. Armed with guns and bolo knives,
the rebels knifed sentries, rushed upon the unarmed American
soldiers, and slaughtered fifty of them.

Days of panic followed. Fear spread through the Philippines
that the incident might mean the start of another full insurrection. Americans in Manila armed themselves to walk to
their offices and militarists called for suspending the powers
of civil government. "The Army has been completely stam-
peded by the Samar affair," Taft reported to Washington.
General Chaffee had put mounted patrols to "running about
through Manila at night" and was making "alarming statements that we were standing on a volcano." Such an attitude,
Taft complained, played into the hands of those who sought
to exploit the Philippines. He said both Army and Navy
officers were spreading "rumors of insurrection in the most
peaceful provinces."

President Roosevelt ended some of the uncertainty by
declaring there would be no change in McKinley's program
for civil government of the Philippines. There would be no
additional troops sent in and no fresh military controls.
Governor Taft, he said, had his full confidence as well as his
praise for the work already done. Taft kept calm and proved
himself right and the Army wrong. There was no new insurrection and the immediate panic gradually died. But back in
the United States, as well as among some American businessmen in Manila who resented restrictions on their attempts
to exploit Philippine resources for profit, there were continu-

ing demands for a "get tough" policy that would end all the "nonsense" of protecting Philippine rights.

Exhausted, Taft was stricken with what first was diagnosed as an attack of tropical fever, and then as a serious abdominal abscess. On October 27, he was carried out of Malacanan Palace on a stretcher and was taken to an Army hospital for an immediate operation. For three days there was fear of gangrene and it was seriously thought that he might die. The wound slowly healed, but a second operation had to be performed, and he was far from well. In Washington, President Roosevelt arranged for Taft to take a leave of absence so he could return to the United States and recuperate.

Taft was reluctant to leave with conditions in the Philippines as they were, but the President overrode his objections by telling him his presence in Washington was urgently needed so he could testify before a Senate committee about to begin hearings into the government's Philippine policies. Still weak, Taft sailed from Manila with Nellie and the children on Christmas Eve, 1901, spent most of the voyage to San Francisco resting in a deck chair, and after a brief visit home to Cincinnati, where Nellie's mother had just died, arrived in Washington at the end of January to testify before the Senate.

He was under searching cross-examination in the Senate committee room for three weeks, answering questions for hours at a time, prodded by militarists, superpatriots, those who demanded immediate Philippine independence, and by Democrats who tried to turn the hearings into a political attack against the Republican administrations. Although Taft complained that the Senators were wasting so much time "asking fool questions" that he was tempted to pack up and leave, he acquitted himself well.

Taft told the committee it was the duty of the United States to establish in the Philippines "a government suited to the present possibilities of the people, which shall gradually change, conferring more and more right upon the people to govern themselves, thus educating them in self-government, until their knowledge of government, their knowledge of liberty, shall be such that further action may be taken either by giving them statehood or by making them a quasi-independent government like Canada or Australia, or if they desire it, independence."

The committee hearings also aroused public feelings over one of the touchiest unsolved problems in the Philippines, the question of what was to be done about the so-called "friar's lands." Taft had been wrestling with it since he first arrived in the islands. Among the deep causes of the Filipino resentment against Spanish rule had been the domination of village life by some of the friars of Catholic religious orders who had been the "political bosses" of many towns under the Spanish regime. The churchmen often had dictated town policies, decided how public money should be spent, influenced the choice of officials, and were blamed for many of the miseries that led to the uprising under rebel leader Aguinaldo. Most Filipinos were loyal and devoted Catholics and their feelings were not against the Church, but against those friars who, in Taft's words, gratified "their desire for money and power and other things."

During the long years of Spanish rule the friars had acquired more than 400,000 acres of the richest and most fertile farm lands in the islands, upon which some 60,000 natives worked as tenants, paying what many felt were excessive rents to their friar landlords. When Aguinaldo came to lead the rebel movement, he declared their lands confiscated. Many priests were captured and imprisoned by the rebels, fifty were slain, and others fled their lands, so that no rents had been paid on the properties since. But under the peace treaty with Spain all property rights in the Philippines were guaranteed. Taft and the commissioners had decided that legally the friars had clear and rightful title to their lands. Yet to restore them to the friars and to let them return to their holdings against the will of the people was impossible.

While Taft was in Washington, President Roosevelt discussed the problem with him at a White House conference and agreed to his suggestion that an American representative should be sent directly to Rome to attempt some settlement with the Vatican. The President told him, "You'll have to go to Rome yourself."

The President's announcement that Taft would head a committee to negotiate with the Vatican raised protests from Protestants who charged that the mission would amount to American diplomatic recognition of the Vatican, and from Catholics who were unhappy over what some felt was government interference with Church affairs in the Philippines. The religious controversy grew so strong that the government had to issue a statement that the mission "will not in any sense or degree be diplomatic in its nature, but will be purely a business matter of negotiation." Nevertheless Taft was put on a political tightrope where a misstep could cost the administration the support of thousands of voters.

He arrived in Italy late in May, 1902, and had the first of two audiences with Pope Leo XIII on June 5. Attired in full evening dress, Taft and his committee were ushered through "I know not how many rooms" and finally to a small chamber "where we found the Pope seated on a little throne." He described the Pope as lively despite his extreme age, and after an exchange of pleasantries they got down to an hour's discussion of the friar's lands.

Problems had been created, Taft told the Pope, by the transfer of the Philippines from Catholic Spain to the United States, with its policy of strict separation of church and state; the United States treated all religions alike and aimed to be in every way friendly to the Catholic Church. He said America was anxious to settle the problems by purchase of the lands at a price to be fixed by arbitration, and had no desire to judge the "justice or injustice" of Filipino hatred toward some of the monastic orders. Instead, the government hoped for an agreement that would substitute priests from other areas for the Spanish friars.

A committee of Cardinals was appointed to consider the American proposals and while no immediate agreement was reached, the way was opened for further negotiations in Manila between Taft and an apostolic delegate. The Manila negotiations went on for more than a year, during which Pope Leo XIII died and Pope Pius X took his place. Finally, in November, 1903, a price of about $7,540,000 was decided upon. Congress authorized the Philippine government to raise the money by issuing bonds; the lands were bought from the Church and gradually were sold in small parcels on easy terms to some 50,000 new Filipino landowners. The Spanish clerics were never formally recalled by the Vatican, but their influence waned. Many left the islands and others, including many American priests, took their places.

Taft was given a hero's welcome when he returned to the Philippines in August, 1902, after presenting the people's cause in Rome. His homecoming was turned into a spontaneous celebration as crowds jammed the streets of Manila to cheer him. He had become the personal symbol of the hopes of many.

But during that summer and fall all of nature suddenly seemed to turn against the Philippines. A cholera epidemic swept the islands, taking thousands of lives. A virus disease of cattle, the rinderpest, killed farm and work animals. Crops were hit by windstorms and drought, and a fear of famine rose. With farming and trade nearly at a standstill, unemployment in towns and cities also became widespread, and poverty reduced some natives to near starvation.

Taft was struggling to enforce health and quarantine regulations, pleading with Washington for relief funds, and dealing with a hundred other problems that all at once seemed to threaten the success of his new government, when a cablegram from President Roosevelt reached him on October 26. There was a vacancy on the Supreme Court and the President informed him: "I earnestly desire to appoint you. . . . I greatly hope you will accept. Would appreciate early reply."

It was what he had always wanted most, but Taft felt his duty was to remain in the Philippines, and he sent the President an immediate answer, explaining that with the situation in the islands so critical his leaving would create doubt about America's pledges, unrest and lack of confidence. "Great honor deeply appreciated," he cabled Roosevelt. "Look forward to time when I can accept such an offer but even if it is certain that it can never be repeated I must now decline."

Roosevelt was disappointed, but replied that "your refusal on the ground you give makes me admire you and believe in you more than ever." He asked Taft to suggest others who might fill the Court vacancy and said, "I am quite at a loss whom to appoint to the bench in the place I meant for you."

Taft thought it was settled, but soon another letter came from the President. "I am awfully sorry, old man, but after faithful effort for a month to try to arrange matters on the basis you wanted I find I shall have to bring you home and put you on the Supreme Court," he wrote. "I have the greatest confidence in your judgment; but after all, old fellow, if you will permit me to say so, I am President and see the whole field. . . . After the most careful thought, after the most earnest effort to do what you desired and thought best, I have come, irrevocably, to the decision that I shall appoint you to the Supreme Court . . ."

But if Roosevelt could be stubborn, so could Taft. He let some of the Filipino leaders in Manila know how concerned he was about having to leave. The result was an enormous public demonstration the morning of January 10, 1903. Hundreds of natives, carrying flags and banners, massed in front of the palace to shout in both Spanish and English, "We want Taft!"

Prominent Filipinos began making speeches. Even those who had been active in the rebel movement joined in his praise. Newspaper correspondents cabled stories of the demonstrations to the United States. Taft's fellow commissioners informed the President that grave risk would attend Taft's

leaving. A group of most distinguished Filipinos sent a declaration that he was the only man "able to count upon the
cooperation of all political parties" and that "we solemnly
affirm that the feelings of the Philippine people would be
deeply hurt by the departure of Taft." In Washington, the
White House telegraph room was flooded with an outpouring
of messages.

President Roosevelt gave in. He sent a terse cable: "Taft,
Manila—All right, stay where you are. I shall appoint someone else to the Court."

Taft gradually brought the worst of the emergency problems under control and conditions were much improved as
spring came to the Philippines. He looked forward to conducting a census which would prepare for the eventual election of
a Philippine Assembly which would give the people still more
self-government. But his health was troubling him. He was
stricken with amoebic dysentery, a stubborn and sometimes
fatal disease in the Philippines, and doctors warned that it
would be best for him to get out of the islands and return
to the United States. President Roosevelt became concerned
and more determined to bring him back to Washington.

Late in March, Taft received a letter from the President
telling him that Secretary of War Root had decided "he will
have to leave me next fall" and "I want to ask you whether . . .
you cannot come back to take his place." He pointed out that
as Secretary of War, Taft still would be in charge of the
Philippines since they were under administration of the War
Department. Roosevelt said he needed "the aid and comfort
you would be to me not merely as director of the affairs in
the Philippines, but as my counselor and adviser in all the
great questions that come up."

In a warm personal postscript, hand written beneath the
typed letter, Roosevelt wrote: "If only there were three of you!
Then I would have put one of you on the Supreme Court . . .
one of you as Secretary of War . . . and one of you permanently
as governor of the Philippines. No one can quite take your

place as governor; but no one of whom I can now think save only you can take Root's place as Secretary."

Finally, Taft accepted, reluctant to the end to leave the Philippines. He would have until the end of 1903 to finish his work as governor. By then, he told President Roosevelt, he hoped that "we can be said to have finished the foundation work." A "long step" would have been taken toward giving the Filipinos well organized civil government, with a promise of greater future freedoms, although "of course, I cannot hope to leave everything done . . ." He would leave Manila by Christmas to become Secretary of War.

President Roosevelt answered: "Thank heaven you are to be with me."

** CHAPTER **

10

TAFT became far more than Theodore Roosevelt's Secretary of War. Unofficially, he was the President's executive assistant, policy adviser, legal counselor, arbitrator, trouble-fixer, political salesman, personal diplomat, good-will ambassador, and sometimes acting Secretary of State. When Roosevelt was away, Taft ran the whole government as sort of a substitute President. "Things will be all right in Washington," President Roosevelt would say, "I have left Taft sitting on the lid."

Roosevelt grew to have such confidence in Taft that he could discuss things with him he dared not whisper to anyone else, he said, because "when it is really necessary to keep a secret, you and I keep it absolutely." He called Taft a person "I admire more than any other public man," and Taft admired him as much. They had been friends before, but working together they became as close, affectionate and trusting as two men can be.

Like most strong Presidents, Roosevelt had little patience with the restraints of the Constitution, or with Congress or the courts when they thwarted the executive will. The power of the Presidency in Roosevelt's hands was a "big stick" that he waved to frighten all who opposed his policies. Taft, the orderly man of law, more often used the "big chuckle" of tolerance and good will. Although far apart in methods, they were in agreement on basic matters of policy and Taft came to feel that in helping to carry out Roosevelt's program he was seeing his own ideas put into effect.

Taft had come back to Washington from the Philippines at the start of President Roosevelt's 1904 reelection campaign and much to his personal displeasure found himself almost immediately stumping around the country as a political speech-maker. He had been away from active politics so long he doubted his ability, but he proved to be one of the best of the Republican campaigners. His speeches were orthodox and entirely partisan. He condemned Roosevelt's opponent, Alton B. Parker, and the rest of the Democrats, and praised the Republicans as an "affirmative party" to which the nation owed its blessings.

When Roosevelt's overwhelming victory came in November, Taft was pleased and also thoroughly glad that the "campaign nightmare" was over. His own prominence as a campaigner led to newspaper predictions that he would be among leading Republican Presidential candidates in 1908. But with his ambition still fixed upon the Supreme Court, Taft said, "I would not run for President if you guaranteed the office." President Roosevelt also was making statements he would regret, especially his firm pledge to the nation that after this second term he would not be President again. On election night, Roosevelt promised the American people: "Under no circumstances will I be a candidate for or accept another nomination."

The Tafts rented a pleasant old-fashioned house in Washington, which made up in added space for what it lacked in elegance. The Taft children soon were romping through the White House with the young Roosevelts. Taft and Nellie also were frequently there, but Nellie shared little of Taft's personal admiration for Theodore Roosevelt. She resented Roosevelt's influence over her husband, which at times was as strong as her own. Nellie was determined to see Taft become the next President, whether that was what he wanted or not; she wanted to be not merely a guest in the White House, but First Lady.

Taft spent as much time as he could with the children and when he was away his letters were filled with detailed advice about their schoolwork and personal activities. He made sure he was in Washington to take young Charlie and Helen to school on opening day. When his oldest son, Robert, had his first vacation from the Taft School in Connecticut, headed by his uncle Horace, Taft took him on a long walking tour of Washington to visit the important buildings and monuments, and then to lunch at the White House with the President.

But Taft was so often rushing off on some hurried trip that newspapers took to calling him Roosevelt's "traveling secretary" and cartoonists pictured him swinging wildly along behind the President, perspiring, his hat lifted by the wind as he dragged a bulging suitcase. "These cartoons," Nellie wrote, "were rather accurately descriptive of real conditions."

His first major task, in addition to running the affairs of the Philippines from his desk in Washington, was to take charge of building the Panama Canal. While Taft was still in the Philippines, President Roosevelt had seized the land for the canal from Colombia, which had been reluctant to sell, by encouraging a revolution that set up the Republic of Panama. The United States swiftly recognized the new republic so Roosevelt could push through a treaty that gave America the hot, yellow fever ridden isthmus that became the Canal Zone. Panama was paid ten million dollars that Colombia had spurned and a group of bankers pocketed most of another forty million dollars approved by Congress to settle the claims of a private French company which had started to build the canal and finally had given up.

The United States achieved an advantage in naval security it had been seeking since the Spanish-American War, but the land grab added greatly to Latin America's lasting mistrust.

Within the United States some Democrats were outraged by Roosevelt's new "imperialism," but the majority of Americans joined in the enthusiastic cry, "Let the dirt fly!" Almost everybody wanted the canal built in a hurry, but hardly anybody knew where to begin or what kind of a canal to build.

Congress had given President Roosevelt wide powers by specifying that the work was to be under the control of a seven-man Isthmian Canal Commission, appointed by and responsible only to him. But Roosevelt decided, as soon as Taft became Secretary of War, that he should be put in top command of the canal-building job. "The President announced to the Commission," as Taft put it, "that they were to be under me as Secretary of War whether the law provided so or not."

Supervising the construction of the canal, Taft discovered, was enough to take the full time of any executive, even though he was unable to give full time to it. There were enormous engineering, labor and sanitation problems to be overcome, political and financial troubles, disputes over nearly every major and minor policy decision, and frictions, quarrels and personal feelings to be soothed. But the most immediate trouble was that in the fledgling Republic of Panama itself there were threats of a second revolution by Panamanians who feared the United States meant to use its treaty to gobble up their new republic completely.

President Roosevelt decided to send Taft there at once to convince the people that "in asserting the equivalent of sovereignty over the canal strip," the United States meant to exercise "all proper care for the honor and interests . . . of Panama" and was about to confer "a very great benefit by the expenditure of millions of dollars in the construction of the canal."

Taft reached the Canal Zone on November 27, 1904, and went to work to settle the unrest. The treaty had given the United States a zone forty miles across and ten miles wide from Colon to Panama, but had excluded those two cities and their harbors from the zone, without any exact boundaries and with no regulations for dealings between the zone and the Republic of Panama. "We were lying in bed with them," Taft noted, "and we took our part of the bed in the middle." He worked out the major problems, quieted the immediate dangers of revolution, and proved to be such a good salesman of American friendship that the first of many trips he would make to Panama ended with a people's demonstration in his honor and pledges of cooperation with the United States.

During his visit he made his first official inspection of the isthmus with a group of engineers and reported that "the canal did not look much like a canal" and the "prospect of its construction was by no means clear." All along the line of operations the old French machinery "lay buried in pathetic ruin in a tropic jungle." Yellow fever threatened and the actual digging itself would require "the excavation of a mass greater than ever before made in the history of the world."

Rail lines had to be built, docks had to be erected, lands had to be drained and swamps had to be filled in. There was a need for work towns, housing, hospitals, sewage and water systems. Some fifty thousand laborers had to be recruited, union disputes had to be settled, machinery and supplies had to be purchased and shipped. All those things had to be done before the actual building of the canal began. During his four years as Secretary of War, the Panama Canal was Taft's greatest continuing burden.

Against the majority recommendation of an international board of engineering experts that the United States should build a sea-level canal, Taft sided with a minority and with President Roosevelt in favoring a lock-system canal, because it could be built for half as much money in half the time the sea-level project would take and because it would serve larger vessels. Taft acted as the President's parliamentary whip on the measure in the Senate, to win votes for the lock canal and beat down the sea-level measure, and helped put it through Congress.

He stood behind Colonel William Gorgas of the Army

Medical Corps when other sanitary experts were laughing at his theory that the mosquito was responsible for spreading the plague of yellow fever. Taft backed Gorgas firmly in his efforts to dry up the swamps and pools that were mosquito-breeding places, to segregate stricken patients, and to clean up sanitation in the towns and cities. By cleansing the Canal Zone of the dreaded yellow fever, Gorgas insured completion of the canal.

When the original Isthmian Canal Commission proved inefficient because of divided responsibilities, Taft approved a reorganization. He and President Roosevelt decided the building of the canal should be withdrawn from private engineering companies and should be put in charge of Army engineers. Taft had a man in mind for the top canal-building job, an Army engineer who had impressed him greatly when he met him during his first inspection trip in Panama, and so he recommended Major George W. Goethals. Taft informed the President that Goethals was "very able" and would "give his heart and mind to it." Roosevelt accepted Taft's recommendation, the man who was to become the great canal-builder was appointed, and Taft gave Goethals full say in naming his assistants.

Meanwhile Taft was pressed into duty as acting Secretary of State early in 1905 when John Hay was stricken with what was to be a fatal illness. Roosevelt soon took off on a trip that also left Taft in charge of the rest of the government. But with all his other work, Taft did not neglect the Philippines. He kept his promise that in becoming Secretary of War he meant to put their welfare first.

He had testified before Congressional committees and had worked endlessly for the passage of bills to cut tariffs on Philippine products and to develop railroads and reform the currency, only to see many of the measures delayed or killed in Congress by sugar, tobacco and other lobbies. Taft was far from satisfied with the way America's pledges to the

Philippines were being met by Congress, and he was also worried over Japan's intentions toward the Philippines.

He made a bold decision to take a good part of the United States Congress with him on a trip to the Philippines for a firsthand look at what was being accomplished there and to reassure the Filipinos and show the world America still had a vital interest in the islands. President Roosevelt agreed and some thirty influential members of Congress, both Democrats and Republicans, accepted the invitation to go with Taft. The journeying party eventually swelled to more than eighty with the addition of officials and newspaper correspondents; the President even decided to send his popular daughter, Alice Roosevelt, along.

Reporters called Taft the "Noah of a Congressional Ark" when the *S.S. Manchuria* steamed out of San Francisco in July, 1905, for its two-month voyage to the Far East and back. "I doubt if so formidable a Congressional representation ever went so far," he said. "The great advantage to the islands . . . is that hereafter the members of the delegation will always have an interest in the legislation which will come up in respect to the Philippines." Without his harmonizing talents, he easily might have brought back a human cargo of Congressional quarrelers who would have hurt his Philippine program instead of helping it. It was with pride that Taft was able to report afterwards: "We took eighty people with us and came back so harmonious that everyone was able to speak to everyone else."

Despite its serious purposes, the trip took on the air of a sightseeing pleasure junket. Correspondents sent home dispatches of Taft's four-mile daily reducing walks around deck, his more entertaining part in shipboard parties, dances, bridge and poker games, and his presiding over a mock trial as well as taking a hand in a pillow fight. Alice Roosevelt's madcap activities all but stole the show from Taft. She kept the news wires humming by donning glamorous costumes for masquerade balls, showing her ability as an amateur magician with a pack of cards, boldly chain smoking cigarettes, and accepting a dare to plunge fully clothed into the ship's swimming pool.

When the Congressional delegation reached the Philippines, Taft saw to it that they were properly impressed. There were tours, discussions, inspection trips, and a round of receptions, banquets, public demonstrations and speeches. Looking out at a huge crowd that gathered in front of Malacanan Palace to welcome his return, he was deeply moved by the "sea of faces," and said that "every face suggests something of crisis . . . that filled four years of the life that I spent on these islands. . . . I love the noble Filipino people. I admire their courage . . . and least of all do I underestimate their aspirations to become a self-governing people and a nation."

His visit did much to renew Philippine-American friendship, but as important as that was, Taft's trip to the Far East had an even more important hidden purpose, well concealed by all the attention given by the newspapers to other activities. On the way to the Philippines the American visitors had stopped off in Japan. While the Congressmen were sightseeing and correspondents were reporting the glittering social trivia of palace visits, royal receptions, and Alice Roosevelt's entertaining pranks, Taft was carrying out highly secret negotiations with Japan for the President.

President Roosevelt had intervened to end war between Japan and Russia so as to keep international rivalries from exploding into a European war. Japan, long at odds with Russia over Manchuria and Korea, had begun the Russo-Japanese War with a surprise attack on the Russian fleet at Port Arthur in February, 1904. Although the United States had been officially neutral, most Americans strongly sympathized with Japan as Russia suffered disastrous defeats. Victorious Japan, while winning its battles, had almost exhausted its manpower and its money, and the Japanese secretly asked President Roosevelt to act as a mediator in bringing peace.

Roosevelt, who had been working hard for peace, immediately accepted the Japanese bid and finally and almost single-handedly got both Russia and Japan to agree to a peace conference to be held in the United States. Before it was held he wanted to reach some understandings with Japan, so he had Taft stop in Tokyo on his way to the Philippines. Taft had no written instructions from the President. His orders were verbal and no record of them was kept. But on July 27, 1905, he conferred with the Japanese premier, Count Taro Katsura, and the result was what amounted to a secret treaty.

Roosevelt agreed, through Taft, that Japan should achieve its centuries-old ambition to absorb Korea in exchange for a pledge to assure the safety of the Philippines from any threats of Japanese aggression and a promise to uphold the open-door principle of international free trade in the Far East. The agreement to give Japan a free hand in Korea was kept secret until after Roosevelt's death. At the time of his secret conference in Tokyo, Taft cabled an agreed-upon memorandum of the "conversation between prime minister and myself" to Washington, carefully avoiding any direct quotations. He said he had pointed out to Katsura that it would be "difficult, indeed impossible, for the President . . . to enter even an informal understanding without the consent of the Senate" but "appropriate action by the United States could be counted upon . . . just as confidently as if a treaty had been signed."

Roosevelt cabled Taft his prompt approval: "Your conversation with Count Katsura absolutely correct in every respect. Wish you would state to Katsura that I confirm every word you have said."

While Taft went on with his trip to the Philippines, President Roosevelt, with patient tact and diplomatic skill, brought the Japanese and Russian peace delegates together at the American naval base at Portsmouth, New Hampshire, which had been chosen because Washington was too hot for an August conference. The Treaty of Portsmouth, signed September 5, 1905, ended the Russo-Japanese War, and for his services in behalf of peace Roosevelt became the first American honored with the Nobel Peace Prize.

Russia recognized Japan's interests in Korea, ceded the southern half of Sakhalin Island, a railroad and other territorial rights to Japan, and both sides agreed to withdraw military forces from Manchuria. But Japan failed to get $600,000,000 in cash it had demanded as indemnity for the cost of the war and the Japanese people were outraged when they learned the terms. In Tokyo there were riots and demonstrations against America, and in the United States friendly feelings toward Japan quickly began to turn and to produce tensions in Japanese-American relations.

By the time Taft finished his Philippine trip and stopped briefly in Japan again on his way home in October, he found that the Japanese had become so angry with the United States that "instead of being received by great cheering crowds that had said farewell to us in July, I went from the dock to the hotel between closely formed files of a regiment of cavalry."

But while he noted that he had lost some of his faith in both "princes and popular enthusiasm," he remained convinced that his Philippines would remain safe from Japanese aggression, at least for a time, and he headed back to Washington where President Roosevelt urgently needed him for other tasks.

✳✳ CHAPTER ✳✳

11

TAFT knew by early 1906 that he probably could have the next Republican nomination for President if he wanted it, but he kept hoping, for as long as he could, that the Presidency wouldn't happen to him. President Roosevelt, party leaders, close friends, Taft's brothers, and most of all Nellie, were urging him to make an active bid for the nomination. But Nellie wrote that he "paid very little attention and never did he cease to regard a Supreme Court appointment as vastly more desirable than the Presidency."

When John Hay died President Roosevelt wanted to make Taft Secretary of State, but Taft was so involved with all the duties that had been channeled through the War Department that the President decided he had to leave him where he was. Roosevelt talked Elihu Root into returning to Washington to become Secretary of State, and the three men made an unusually effective combination at the head of government. Newspapers dubbed them the "Three Musketeers" and cartoonists pictured them as the swashbuckling characters created by novelist Alexander Dumas: Roosevelt, the gay, high-spirited, brave and quick-tempered D'Artagnan; Root, the gallant and gentlemanly Athos; Taft, the good-hearted and physical giant Porthos. They were greatly amused by the cartoons and for a time signed their notes to each other with the adopted names of the Musketeers.

Taft, the portly Porthos, came back from the Philippines weighing a scale-crushing 320 pounds, but under a doctor's supervision, by strict dieting, horseback riding and other regular exercise, he had dropped seventy pounds in six months, to bring himself to 250, and felt far more alert and efficient.

He had "never been quite so busy," he wrote early in 1906. "I am overwhelmed with work. Philippine matters, Panama Canal matters, Army matters, the disaster at San Francisco . . ." The "disaster" was San Francisco's earthquake and fire, news of which Taft received by way of a White House telephone call after midnight on April 16. He promptly ordered Army tents and supplies rushed into the stricken city and supervised the spending of $2,500,000 for relief work.

But his own life was far more shaken by the personal earthquake of having to decide whether to run for President or to take a place on the Supreme Court. President Roosevelt had promised Taft his active support for the Presidency, if that was what he wanted, but he also had promised the Supreme Court, if that was Taft's choice. Roosevelt wasn't sure where Taft stood, and neither was Taft. The Tafts were in Lakewood, New Jersey, spending a weekend with friends, when Roosevelt phoned from Washington to tell Taft that Associate Justice Henry B. Brown had decided to resign; the President wanted to offer him first chance for the Court seat. Taft told Roosevelt he was interested but would like time to think it over. He was inclined to accept, but Nellie immediately disapproved, saying he would be throwing away an almost certain chance for the Presidency. She argued that if Roosevelt had offered to make him Chief Justice that might be worth considering, but not just a routine place on the Court.

When Taft got back to Washington, he talked it over with the President several times. During one of their private talks, Taft explained that Nellie was "bitterly opposed to my accepting the (Court) position" and had warned him he would be making "the mistake of my life." The President agreed to see

Nellie for him and try to explain the advantages to her. So Nellie went to see Roosevelt. But the President, instead of explaining, apparently found himself doing the listening as Nellie emphatically told him why her husband should refuse the Court appointment. Roosevelt wrote Taft afterwards that he had thought the Court was what he wanted, but that after "a half-hour's talk with your dear wife," he wondered if he had been in error.

Whatever his friend wanted, Roosevelt said, was what he wished to do for him, "but no other man can take the responsibility of deciding for you." Personally, Roosevelt thought Taft "could do most as President," that he was the man most likely to receive the nomination, and "I think the best man to receive it." On the other hand, he "could do very much as an associate justice." And Roosevelt promised that if Taft did become an associate justice now, and there later was an opportunity, he would move him to the center of the bench as Chief Justice. "But it is not a light thing to cast aside the chance of the Presidency . . . it is well to remember that the shadow of the Presidency falls on no man twice, save in most exceptional circumstances."

It was an extremely frank letter. "Now, my dear Will . . . it is a hard choice to make, and you yourself have to make it," Roosevelt went on. "You have two alternatives, each with uncertain possibilities" and "you should decide in accordance with the promptings of your own liking, and of your own belief as to where you can render the service which most appeals to you, as well as which you feel is most beneficial to the nation. No one can with wisdom advise you."

At Taft's request, Roosevelt agreed to make no Supreme Court appointment until the end of the year, but the postponement gave Taft no escape from politics, which he said, "make me sick." The Presidential choice was still two years away, but in 1906 there was a Congressional campaign to be waged and the President once more asked Taft to pack his bags and sell Rooseveltism to the nation.

Taft interrupted a vacation with his family at Murray Bay to go to Bath, Maine, on September 5 and make an address Roosevelt later praised as "the great speech of the campaign." It was a rousing antitrust speech in which Taft upheld Roosevelt's war against the monopolies of wealth and attacked the "evils of misuse and abuse" of the instruments of opportunity "in the hands of the comparatively few." He also alarmed some conservative Republicans by suggesting the possible need for a downward revision of high tariffs.

The speech put the political spotlight directly upon him as a Presidential possibility, but Taft hurriedly retreated to Murray Bay again, hoping for a little more vacation before he went on with the Congressional campaign. He had hardly settled into his big porch chair to enjoy the cool breezes of the St. Lawrence River before President Roosevelt summoned him to Washington, not for a campaign task this time, but to put down a threatened revolution in Cuba.

During the Spanish-American War, the United States had promised never to exercise "sovereignty, jurisdiction or control" over Cuba once it was freed from Spain, but after the war it had qualified its idealistic pledge. To protect millions of dollars of American investments in Cuban properties and to make sure Cuba could maintain a stable government, the United States had adopted a policy of "watchful protection."

It had turned the new Republic of Cuba into what amounted to an American protectorate by forcing the Cubans, under protest, to guarantee the right of the United States to intervene in its affairs, if that ever became necessary to "protect life, property and individual liberty." By early September, 1906, demands were being made for America to intervene to save the tottering government of Cuban President Tomás Palma, whose conservative policies had aroused Cuban liberals to the point of armed revolt. There were charges that Palma's reelection had been rigged and he had asked for the protection of American warships and troops.

With the Congressional campaign underway in the United

States, President Roosevelt hoped to avoid inflaming the feelings of American voters over the touchy issue of Cuban intervention, so he announced that he was sending Taft to Cuba to try to bring about some settlement. His private instructions to Taft were to "do anything that is necessary . . . but try to do it in as gentle a way as possible."

Taft reached Havana on September 19, 1906, to find the island in a state of near anarchy, with only the coast and provincial capitals under the control of President Palma's shaky government, and with an estimated twenty thousand insurgents armed to fight the Cuban federal forces. An uneasy truce held them apart as both sides waited to see what Taft, acting for the United States, would do. He began what he later called "those awful twenty days" of trying to keep the explosive situation from bursting into full revolution.

President Palma and his party officials, who hoped to force the United States into backing them, were dismayed when Taft made it clear that he also wanted to interview leaders of the opposing Liberal party. For several days he held hearings at the American ministry, and came to the conclusion that the Palma government lacked the support of the majority of Cubans, and also that there was little doubt that the Palma faction had "flagrantly and openly used and abused its power to carry the elections." But he was convinced that Palma himself, although "obstinate and difficult," was personally "honest and patriotic," and that there was no one man on the Liberal side who could pull all the Cuban factions together as President.

Taft presented Palma and his party leaders with a compromise. Palma was to remain in office, but his cabinet was to resign so a new cabinet could include Liberals. New elections, carefully supervised, were to be held immediately to provide Liberals with an honest chance to win seats in the Cuban congress, and the Cuban constitution was to be amended to give the people greater voice in city administrations. President Palma refused to accept the terms and insisted that either his entire government stayed in power or he would end the government. He finally carried out his threat by calling a joint session of the Cuban congress. Palma and his cabinet resigned and the congress refused to name any successor as President.

Taft's duty then was to prevent full revolution. On September 29, with American Marines landing and a large force of Army troops ready to move in, Taft issued a proclamation that Cuba had been "left without a government at a time when great disorder prevails" and that "to restore order and protect life and property" a provisional government "is hereby established." He named himself the temporary Provisional Governor of Cuba, pledged that the Cuban flag would still fly, and that when full peace and public confidence were restored elections would be held to determine who should take office to continue "the permanent government of the Republic."

He appealed to the people to cooperate, and insurgents began to turn in their arms. He moved into the Cuban Presidential Palace, set up a governmental authority to work with city and regional officials, and issued decrees which allowed Cubans to carry on a good part of the routine of government. On October 3, President Roosevelt appointed Charles E. Magoon, previously governor of the Canal Zone, to relieve Taft in Cuba, and ten days later Magoon arrived and took over as provisional governor.

American occupation lasted nearly three years, but Taft lost no time in leaving Havana in 1906. He wrote his brother Charles that "to get away from this" he would even face the ordeals of American politics. He had pretty well made up his mind that he "couldn't escape" the coming Presidential nomination, and he returned to the United States to resume the 1906 battle for a Republican Congress that he had interrupted to prevent revolution in Cuba.

✳✳ CHAPTER ✳✳

12

TAFT traveled across the country and back in the fall of
1906, speaking several times a day to enthusiastic crowds
to urge the election of Republicans to Congress to support
President Roosevelt's program. He insisted that his private
talks with dozens of Republican party leaders along the way
had nothing to do with any personal ambitions, but he was
well aware of the efforts others were making to put him in the
White House.

Among possible Republican contenders Taft himself was
the last to be convinced that Taft would be the best candidate.
But his resistance gradually wore away under family pressure,
President Roosevelt's encouragement, Nellie's insistence, and
the appeals of Republican leaders. When his brother, Charles,
began to set up headquarters in Cincinnati and in Washington,
Taft asked if it was necessary to start so soon. Despite his
dislike for politics, however, he knew if he was to be nominated that delegates pledged to him had to be lined up and
that state and county leaders and the city bosses had to be
won to his support.

President Roosevelt interrupted Taft's pre-convention maneuvering in the fall of 1907 to send him on a three-month
trip around the world as an American ambassador of peace.

He was to visit Japan to cool outraged feelings that had brought Japan and the United States close to war. Then he was to go to the Philippines for the opening session of the Philippine National Assembly, the new legislature to which Filipinos had just elected their first delegates. After that, he was to visit Russia, to show the Russians, who had just been at war with Japan, that America wanted to be friendly with everybody.

California had been whipped into a frenzy of racial antagonism toward the Japanese by fears of the "Yellow Peril," aroused by sensational newspaper stories that the flood of immigrant Japanese laborers into the West Coast was merely a prelude to Japanese ambitions to take jobs from Americans, capture the state, and then invade California. Newspapers were printing wild rumors that the Japanese were poised to land on the beaches, that a "horde of Yellow Men" was ready to strike overland from Mexico, and that the entire coast was in peril.

Japan was still angry at the United States over President Roosevelt's settlement of the Russo-Japanese War, which many Japanese blamed for cheating them of the full rewards of military victory. Anti-American riots in Tokyo had been followed by open clashes off Alaska between Japanese seal hunting boats and American patrols. When the city of San Francisco passed a law to ban Japanese children from its public schools in order to segregate them from white Americans, and when Californians began to attack Japanese shops and to demand an act of Congress to keep all Japanese out of the United States, Japan's feelings turned to outrage. The Japanese government formally protested to the United States against San Francisco's school ban.

President Roosevelt, fearing not only war with Japan but a conflict which would involve most of the European powers because of Far Eastern alliances, got San Francisco to halt its segregation of Japanese school children, warned Californians that he would use all the forces of government necessary to protect the rights of Japanese citizens, and had Congress pass a law which would let him negotiate with Japan to limit the immigration of Japanese laborers into the United States. He then sent the American Navy on a practice cruise into Far Eastern waters to demonstrate America's naval power, and at the same time sent Taft on his journey to soothe the Japanese.

Along with the other missions of his many-purposed trip, Taft almost incidentally launched his own pre-convention campaign for the Presidential nomination. Late in August, 1907, he began making his way slowly westward across the United States and also building political strength in private talks with party leaders. He delivered so many speeches his voice went hoarse and he shook hands until he "groaned with the ache" in his fingers.

Nellie thought Taft should resign from Roosevelt's cabinet to divorce himself from too close an association with the President, but Taft answered that "my strength is largely as his friend." She was suspicious that Roosevelt might change his mind and seek another term, and she warned Taft against making "any more speeches on the Roosevelt policies" because "you are simply aiding and abetting the President in keeping things stirred up." Taft ignored such advice, although he often smilingly admitted that "Nellie is the real political boss of the family."

Nellie and their ten-year-old son Charlie joined Taft at Yellowstone National Park for his world trip, and they arrived in Japan late in September to become palace guests of the Emperor. Taft immediately went to work to smooth Japanese-American relations at an official banquet given for him in Tokyo, where he made a speech designed for consumption at home as well as in Japan. Both nations, he pointed out, had been good friends and there were no differences between them that could not be settled by "statesmen of honor, sanity and justice." Skillfully he praised the heroism of Japanese armies, saying that the Russo-Japanese treaty had established Japan as one of the world's great powers, and that everyone knew Japan didn't want another war that would interfere with its plans to develop Korea. He discounted the racial disturbances in California as "a little cloud that has come over the sunshine of a fast friendship of fifty years."

In conferences with Japan's Foreign Minister Hayashi, he tried to make it clear that the outbreaks in California were caused by sensational journalism and did not represent the true feelings of the American people toward Japan. From Hayashi, he got assurances that most Japanese people were not interested in emigration to the United States and that Japan would be willing to restrict emigration if it did not involve making an official concession as part of a treaty which would admit "inequality with other races."

The result was the eventual working out of a "gentlemen's agreement," whereby Japan agreed to limit the issuing of passports for Japanese laborers to go to the United States in exchange for an American promise that the United States would not officially exclude Japanese immigrants. In talks with Hayashi and with the Emperor, Taft also was assured that Japan was "most anxious to avoid war" for any reason with the United States. Taft's visit, in addition to laying the groundwork for an informal treaty, helped greatly to quiet war fears at home and to convince Japanese officials that America was interested in peace.

With the tides of war turned, at least for a time, Taft went on to the Philippines and spoke at the opening of the National Assembly in Manila, celebrating with his "brown brothers" their new freedom to elect their own lawmakers as part of the gradual self-government he had promised the Filipinos as governor. However, he was almost bluntly honest in telling them full Philippine independence was still a long time off. "They did not like the truth," he said afterwards, but "one must be strictly truthful with them in letter and spirit . . ." There were banquets, parties, dances and receptions, and inspection trips to projects Taft had started years before. He was proud to see many of them completed "and proving to be as useful as we had hoped they would be."

The Tafts left the Philippines in November, and reached Vladivostok after a rough sea voyage. They boarded the Trans-Siberian Railway for a twelve-day trip across Siberia. The family arrived in Moscow late on a Saturday night, had the Kremlin specially opened for a Sunday visit, and attended a ballet performance at the opera in Taft's honor. He spoke at an official banquet before taking a midnight train to St. Petersburg. There he had three days of conferences with Russian officials, some of whom pleasantly recalled the years when Taft's father had been American Minister to Russia, and an audience and palace luncheon with Czar Nicholas II.

From Russia, Taft went on to Berlin for the trip home. When his ship reached Plymouth, England, he received the sad news that his mother had died on December 7. The funeral was held before he could get back to the United States, but he went directly to Cincinnati to put a wreath on her grave.

If there was any lingering doubt as to the man President Roosevelt had chosen to succeed him, the President ended it in January, 1908, by passing the word to newspaper correspondents that Taft was his definite choice. And Taft made it clear that "I agree heartily and earnestly in the policies which have come to be known as the Roosevelt policies." As the campaign went into high gear, it was fairly certain that the nomination would be his, but delegate pledges still had to be nailed down. Taft journeyed as far west as Omaha on a final pre-convention speaking trip in April, then made another quick visit to the Panama Canal to solve some troubles that President Roosevelt decided were in need of his personal attention, and hurried home to deliver speeches in the Eastern states.

When the Republican National Convention met at the Chicago Coliseum on June 16, the Roosevelt-Taft forces were in firm control of the party machine and real opposition to

Taft no longer existed. Presided over by Roosevelt's friend, Massachusetts' Senator Henry Cabot Lodge, the convention did its work according to orders from the White House. The usual disputes over the admission of delegates were settled in favor of Taft supporters, and he got most of the planks he and Roosevelt wanted written into the party platform. There were two wild demonstrations for Roosevelt, one of which lasted forty-nine minutes, and for a brief time it seemed possible that Roosevelt, despite his pledge to the nation never to run again, might be nominated by a stampede of delegates. But Chairman Lodge kept tight control and steered the convention toward its predetermined goal.

Nellie, who was with Taft and a few close friends in Washington listening to convention bulletins that came by long-distance telephone, was annoyed by the demonstrations for Roosevelt, and to those who were there, Taft appeared far less excited than she was. Several times he left his office on official business. When he finally was overwhelmingly nominated, as expected on the first ballot, he seemed pleased but not overjoyed.

Roosevelt issued a statement of congratulations which informed the nation, in effect, that a vote for Taft was a vote for Roosevelt. "I have known him intimately for many years and . . . throughout that time we have worked for the same object, with the same purposes and ideals," he said. "I do not believe there can be found in the whole country a man so well fitted to be President."

On June 30, Taft resigned as Secretary of War to devote all his time to the election campaign, and went with Nellie to Hot Springs, Virginia, to rest and prepare the acceptance speech he was to deliver in Cincinnati. In the speech, which Roosevelt read in advance and pronounced "admirable," Taft set not only the keynote for his campaign, but clearly outlined ways in which his Presidency would differ from Roosevelt's.

"The chief function of the next administration, in my

judgment, is distinct from, and a progressive development of that which has been performed by President Roosevelt," he said. Explaining that he hoped to "complete and perfect the machinery," he promised that a span of quiet was to follow the years of Roosevelt tumult. "The practical, constructive and difficult work . . . of those who follow Mr. Roosevelt," Taft said, "is to devise the ways and means by which the high level of business integrity and obedience to law . . . may be maintained and departures from it restrained without undue interference with legitimate business."

Meanwhile the Democrats, in a July convention at Denver, had nominated William Jennings Bryan for his third and last attempt to capture the Presidency. Bryan, despite his oratorical skill, proved to be a rather ineffective campaigner who confused the issues by approving of much of what Roosevelt had done, but claiming that Roosevelt hadn't gone far enough and that the Democrats could do it better.

Taft, after getting his campaign off to a good start, sat back for a while and didn't really begin stumping the country in earnest until September. Roosevelt pleaded with him to "make the fight aggressively." He told Taft, "Do not *answer* Bryan; attack him! Don't let *him* make the issues. . . . Hit them hard, old man!" To keep a political audience from nodding, Roosevelt advised him, he had to paint things in broad strokes "with streaks of blue, yellow and red to catch the eye."

But Taft couldn't make himself into an imitation Roosevelt. He told his advisers that "I cannot be more aggressive than my nature makes me." Having been a judge, he realized that his approach was still too often judicial. "I can't call names and I can't use adjectives when I don't think the case calls for them," he said, "so you will have to get along with that kind of a candidate . . . and if the people don't like that kind of a man, then they have got to take another."

Most of Taft's speeches were far too long. Despite Roosevelt's urgings he was unable to dramatize issues to capture public attention. Yet his laughter, his personality, his ability to say what he thought and to state his views honestly, did please audiences. Sometimes his humor was too subtle, but when he chuckled over a joke, others did too.

He wound up his last campaign trip the morning of election day and returned to Cincinnati to the home of his brother, Charles, to wait out the returns with Nellie, the family, and a group of friends. The first returns from New York indicated victory and by midnight the result was fairly certain. Long before the final electoral vote of 321 for Taft and 162 for Bryan came in, a victory crowd gathered outside the house.

A band played and Taft stepped into the glare of red fire from torches to acknowledge the greeting. The fifty-one-year-old next President of the United States was a very tired man. He had been talking for forty days, his voice was almost gone, and his face was deeply lined. He briefly expressed the hope that his administration would be "a worthy successor of that of Theodore Roosevelt," and then with a smile pleaded that he be allowed to get some rest. While the telegraph still ticked off its incomplete reports in a downstairs parlor, Taft went up to bed.

** CHAPTER **

13

THE Weather Bureau had predicted clear skies for Taft's inauguration on March 4, 1909, but howling winds swirled snow through the streets of Washington. The Tafts had spent the night at the White House at President Roosevelt's invitation, but the evening had been strained, uneasy, and less than a success.

Roosevelt, giving up the power and glory of the Presidency, wished he could keep it; Taft, taking it from him, knew the decisions would now have to be his. Outwardly they went on trying to preserve their old relationship, but it had changed. Eventually their political hatred for each other would be as strong as their friendship once had been.

Together, they rode in the same carriage to the Capitol, where all hope of an outdoor ceremony had been abandoned. In the Senate chamber Chief Justice Melville Fuller, in whose shoes Taft wished he were standing, administered the Oath of Office. The new twenty-seventh President of the United States delivered his inaugural address in a slow and solemn voice. He praised Roosevelt's reform administration, and said that his policy would be "to render the reforms lasting."

When Taft had finished, former President Roosevelt was the first to step forward and shake his hand. "God bless you, old man," he boomed. "It is a great state document." With that, his eyes glistening behind their glasses, Roosevelt strode out to a waiting carriage that would take him to the railroad station. He was determined to remove himself from Washington so as to give Taft a free hand while he went off to Africa on a hunting trip.

Nellie, despite some opposition from the inaugural committee, had her way and proudly set precedent by being the first of First Ladies to sit with her husband in the carriage that took them from the Capitol back to the White House. When Taft was asked how it felt to enter the place that would be his home for the next four years, he said, "I hardly know yet. When I hear someone say 'Mr. President,' I look around expecting to see Roosevelt."

But Nellie paused in the White House doorway. "I stood for a moment," she later wrote, "over the great brass seal bearing the national coat-of-arms, which is sunk in the floor in the middle of the entrance hall. 'The Seal of the President of the United States,' I read around the border, and now— that meant my husband!"

During the four months between his election and inauguration Taft had made decisions that were to turn his administration sharply from the methods Roosevelt had followed. Roosevelt had used the Presidency as an ax, to cut at the roots of special privilege in America and had planted new seeds of social justice. Taft's weapon was to be the law book, not the ax. "Mr. Roosevelt's function has been to preach a crusade against certain evils. He has aroused the public to demand reform," Taft wrote. "It becomes my business to put that reform into legal execution."

He had caused hard feelings among ardent Roosevelt supporters by telling most of the old cabinet members their services would not be needed because he wanted his own cabinet, made up mainly of lawyers, who instead of making dramatic gestures would be able to get reforms enacted as law. He named moderate Republicans since he felt Congress "would certainly oppose recommendations made by a cabinet consisting of the more radical members of the party."

To some Roosevelt men, anything Taft did that was different was wrong. Roosevelt had inspired such a devoted personal following that there were those who resented even minor changes. "To hear them talk," Captain Archie Butt, the senior White House aide, said, "one would think that Mr. Roosevelt was being driven out of the White House by Mr. Taft."

Taft also had to contend with the image of the man who had been among the boldest and most colorful of American Presidents. Bound by his judicial outlook and his belief that the Constitution placed strict limitations upon the powers of the President, it was not in Taft's nature to take impulsive short cuts or to indulge in the Roosevelt thunder that made headlines and captured public opinion. He soon admitted there was no use "trying to be William Howard Taft with Roosevelt's ways."

He was a disappointment to Washington correspondents. From the beginning, his press relations were poor. Unable to handle the press as Roosevelt had, he felt uneasy talking to reporters, took few into confidence, and made little use of "planted" stories or of indirect methods of "leaking" information that would put across his views. Correspondents, finding they couldn't get much news from White House sources, got it elsewhere, often from opponents of the administration, and Taft's best work was ignored while his errors were seized upon and magnified.

Taft had hoped for a period of political tranquility when he became President, but he had inherited a Republican party at war with itself. A fighting group of younger Republicans, mostly from the West and Midwest, had started to revolt against the combination of politics and big business that had been the party's strength for half a century. The insurgents were Republicans who had come up into Congress the hard way, by battling for liberal reforms in their own states, a small group at first, but noisy, shrewd and determined. Behind them were a growing number of factory workers, farmers, cattlemen and miners, alarmed by the rising costs of living, who blamed Wall Street and Eastern capitalists for "milking the cow" of prosperity that was fed by the West.

When Taft took office, the primary aim of the insurgent revolt was to break the almost dictatorial power of their own party's conservative boss of Congress, Speaker of the House Joseph Cannon, who had been building his political command since Illinois voters he impressed with his homespun doctrines first sent him to Congress back in 1873. "Uncle Joe" Cannon chewed black cigars, told dirty stories, quoted the Bible, and presented himself to the people at home as a plain farmer, but in Congress the crudities dropped from him and he was a skilled and sophisticated master of intricate political maneuvering.

When he became Speaker of the House in 1903, Cannon used the office to make himself the most powerful "czar" Congress had ever known. He appointed all the committees, removed members who would not do his bidding, cut off debate, silenced opposition, and as chairman of the vital Committee on Rules saw to it that Congress considered only bills that he approved. He had contempt for most reform measures as well as for rebellious Republicans who wanted to change things. "The Speaker stands pat," he said, "on his declaration that this country is a hell of a success!"

A group of about thirty Republican Congressmen finally decided to try to strip Cannon of his power by combining with the Democrats to command a voting majority in the House. Taft, before his inauguration, was ready to join in the battle and if Roosevelt had given the word he probably would have declared himself against Cannon. But Roosevelt urged him to be cautious. Since "four-fifths of the Republicans want Cannon," Roosevelt wrote him, "I do not believe it would be well to have him in the position of the sullen and hostile floor leader bound to bring your administration to grief." Instead, Roosevelt arranged for Taft to come to Washington and have a long talk with Cannon.

Taft's main concern as President-elect was to win the support of Congress, which seemed impossible without Cannon's help. So, at Roosevelt's request, he saw "Uncle Joe," and came away with Cannon's promise to cooperate. Reporters made sensational news of the fact that Taft and arch-conservative Cannon had reached a working agreement and the insurgents, who until then had hoped Taft would throw his Presidential prestige on their side, considered the announcement a "death blow" to their cause.

When the Speakership came to a vote in March, 1909, just after Taft had been inaugurated, twenty-four Republicans broke with their party and joined Democrats in the attempt to unseat Cannon, but Cannon won reelection as Speaker by a large House majority. The fight, however, had just begun. A year later, the Republican insurgents renewed the attack and got enough support from Democrats to end Cannon's control over the Rules Committee. Cannon was allowed to remain as Speaker, but was no longer the all-powerful "czar" of the House. He had lost his power to "rubber-stamp" legislation and could not prevent open debate.

The insurgents had won their battle without Taft. He had sacrificed their belief in him for the help he thought Cannon might give his legislative program. Many of the insurgents who were Roosevelt men accused Taft of "betraying" Roosevelt's crusade against combinations of wealth and politics, and Taft's troubles over conservation programs soon increased their bitterness.

Among those Taft had decided not to keep in his cabinet was Roosevelt's Secretary of the Interior, James Garfield, the son of President Garfield, a close friend of Roosevelt's and a strong supporter of his conservation policies. Roosevelt had been effective in protecting mineral and timber rights and the public lands from those who tried to take them over for private profit, but he had carried out his reforms by issuing sweeping executive orders and by delegating authority to others who worried as little as he did over legal technicalities or the will of Congress.

Taft firmly believed in conserving the nation's natural resources, but he also believed that conservation programs had to be based on law and not on executive commands, because what one President did another might just as easily undo. He meant to enact his own conservation plan within the framework of acts of Congress. "We have a government of limited power under the Constitution," he said, "and we have got to work out our problems on the basis of law."

When Taft replaced Garfield as Secretary of the Interior with Richard Ballinger, a former land office commissioner, the cabinet change displeased an even closer friend of Roosevelt's, the Chief of the United States Forest Service, Gifford Pinchot, who was recognized by almost everyone, including Taft, as the nation's leading conservationist. Pinchot and Garfield had worked well together, but Pinchot had little use for Ballinger. He also was unhappy over the fact that Roosevelt was no longer President and Taft was. Ever since Roosevelt had been governor of New York, Pinchot had been master of his conservation policies and his personal admiration for Roosevelt amounted to worship. Under Roosevelt he had been given almost free-handed power for eight years over the vast domain of all the national forests of the United States.

Taft admired Pinchot's achievements and was "glad to have him in the government," but he made it clear that he intended to nullify any orders by Pinchot that were not within the law. Although their relations were outwardly cordial, Taft soon was writing privately that Pinchot was too "willing to camp outside the law to accomplish his beneficent purposes" and that "I have told him so to his face."

With considerable success, Taft managed to get Congress to pass laws that gave the President clear authority to conserve lands that previously had been protected only by executive order. Under such laws, he reserved oil and coal lands as well as forests, and set aside great national reserves in the

Appalachians and in the Western states. He pushed through large appropriation bills for irrigation projects and later established the Bureau of Mines as official guardian of the nation's mineral wealth. But despite that, he became publicly branded as a foe of conservation, a destroyer of Roosevelt's program, and a protector of wealthy interests trying to defraud the country of its natural resources.

The public uproar grew out of an Alaskan coal lands controversy, which Pinchot helped turn into a national scandal to discredit Interior Secretary Ballinger and Taft's administration. Ballinger, after consulting the Attorney General, had approved the claims of some prospectors to a small area of remote coal lands despite the suspicions of a special investigator for the land office, Louis Glavis, that it was part of a conspiracy by wealthy capitalists to defraud the nation of vast deposits of coal. Although Glavis was unable to produce definite evidence, he made the case a personal crusade, carried his suspicions to Pinchot, and convinced him that property "valued at millions" was in danger. Pinchot had some of his assistants in the Forest Service help Glavis prepare a muckraking article for *Collier's Weekly,* accusing Secretary Ballinger of criminal complicity.

Millionaires, the magazine charged, were reaching out for the nation's coal, and Ballinger "with reckless immorality" was a "tricky, furtive and menacing" man who was working against the "interests of the people whom he is supposed to represent." Led by honestly concerned conservationists, newspapers picked up the cry, making it seem as if all of Alaska was about to be "stolen." There were editorial demands that Taft fire Ballinger immediately or share the blame for "protecting a criminal."

Convinced after an investigation that Ballinger had done nothing wrong, Taft refused to dismiss him. He said, "If I were to turn Ballinger out, in view of his innocence . . . I should be a white-livered skunk. I don't care how it affects my administration."

Instead, Taft fired Glavis, and privately appealed to Pinchot not to take "any hasty action" because of his feelings against Ballinger. Pinchot's answer was to write a public letter to a member of the Senate, defending Glavis and his own assistants who had helped with the *Collier's* article, repeating the charge of fraud, and warning that he did not intend to let President Taft punish anybody.

With his Presidential authority openly challenged, Taft was forced to remove Pinchot from office. "By your own conduct you have destroyed your usefulness as a helpful subordinate of the government," Taft wrote, accusing him of using his position to make "an improper appeal to Congress and the public" implying that the President and Secretary of the Interior were involved in fraud. Taft said he could overlook the personal attack upon himself, but it was his duty to maintain proper respect for the Presidency "on the part of my subordinates" and to uphold the executive branch of the government.

To many Americans, Pinchot was conservation, and his firing seemed to confirm the worst of the charges made against the administration. Newspapers heatedly denounced Taft. The *Louisville Courier-Journal* charged: "For the first time in the history of the country a President of the United States has openly proclaimed himself a friend of thieves and the enemy of honest men . . . by the executive order removing Gifford Pinchot from office."

Ballinger demanded a Congressional investigation which later cleared him, and indirectly Taft's administration, but it also served to give the case more publicity. A year later, to save Taft further embarrassment, Ballinger resigned, although Taft wrote that never had there been "such an unjust conspiracy against a man." But much of the public believed the charges, and to the friends of Theodore Roosevelt the firing of Gifford Pinchot seemed proof that Taft had turned his back on the man who had chosen him as President.

** CHAPTER **

14

PRESIDENT TAFT opened a political Pandora's box from which his Presidency never recovered when he called Congress into special session in March, 1909, to revise the tariff law. Republicans in McKinley's administration had pushed tariffs to the highest levels in history and Taft had campaigned for election on a promise to lower them. In the months before he took office he worked with Congressional leaders to reduce duties on imported products so competition would cut prices Americans had to pay for many things they needed to buy. Just as he had cooperated with Joe Cannon in the House, Taft sought support of the Republican boss of the Senate, autocratic millionaire Nelson Aldrich of Rhode Island. Like Cannon, Aldrich was a high tariff man, but Taft expected to win them both over to reasonable tariff reforms for the sake of the party's political future.

His strategy in the beginning was to seek cooperation, not argument, and to adopt a policy of non-interference as far as Congress was concerned. He kept a watchful eye on debate as tariff hearings began, but brought no White House pressure to bear. The strategy seemed to work at first. The House passed and sent on to the Senate a bill that did contain substantial tariff rate reductions. It came "as near complying with our promises as we can hope," Taft said, and "contains much of what I approve."

But in the Senate, he did not succeed. Boss Aldrich put loyalty to his fellow millionaires first and was not about to go along with sweeping downward tariff revisions. Aldrich made short work of the reductions recommended by the House and rewrote the bill to suit himself. By the time it emerged from his Senate Finance Committee, duties had been increased on six hundred items. Aldrich's steamroller tactics brought the Senate insurgents into open revolt. They delayed the bill's passage in debates that thundered all through the spring and into summer. But Aldrich still controlled the party majority. Against the insurgent fury, he finally ram-rodded the bill through the Senate, with some eight hundred amendments riding on it as it went to the conference com-mittee of both houses for the final battle to reach a com-promise.

Taft hoped the House members of the conference com-mittee would battle down the Senate increases. But he didn't expect that "Uncle Joe" Cannon would "betray" him by packing the committee. Cannon named four die-hard high tariff men to represent the House, men who obviously would vote against the House's own version of the bill. Angry and disillusioned, Taft abandoned his policy of non-interference. Too late he turned the full pressures of the Presidency upon Cannon and Aldrich to demand and get some lower rates. Taft brought down duties on shoes and leather, coal, iron ore, lumber, and some other basic items, reduced some below the high increases the Senate wanted, but lost the fight on other important products. He finally decided he had gotten all the reductions Congress would accept. Convinced that he had done the best he could under the circumstances, Taft signed the bill on August 9, 1909.

Almost incidentally he also changed the future tax struc-ture of the United States. During the tariff battle, the Senate insurgents made an attempt to attach a general income tax to the bill. Taft was in favor of an income tax, but not in the form of an act of Congress because the Supreme Court had declared such an act illegal in 1895. Another attempt by Congress to enact an income tax would mean a direct challenge to the Supreme Court.

What Taft advocated instead was submitting the income tax to the people as a Constitutional amendment to be approved by the states. He sent an income tax message to Congress, calling for the adoption of a joint resolution to amend the Constitution. At the same time, to raise immediate tax money, he asked Congress to put a separate tax on the incomes of corporations.

Taft then invited Aldrich and the Senate Finance Committee to the White House and convinced them they had to accept his package or face the threat of an immediate income tax enacted by Congress. Aldrich was convinced the income tax would never get through the states so he finally agreed to accept the corporation tax in the hope that it would help to sidetrack the income tax forever. Taft had the corporation tax drafted so as to give "a kind of Federal supervision over corporations" by providing for tax returns that would "secure valuable information" about how they conducted their business and how they were structured financially. His careful drawing-up of the law later helped government investigators prepare antitrust suits.

Both houses meanwhile sped through approval of Taft's income tax plan and adopted a resolution to submit to the states the Sixteenth Amendment, granting Congress the power "to lay and collect taxes on incomes, from whatever source derived." Despite Aldrich's belief that the states would never adopt it, they did, although final ratification didn't come until Taft's last months as President.

Taft also gained what he considered another victory during the tariff battle by taking the first step to settle the nation's future tariff problems by expert study. He saw to it that the tariff bill allowed the President to hire three expert economists as advisers. Then, as his own creation, he formed the first tariff board to bring some order out of the general confusion over tariff schedules, and appointed a Yale economics professor as its first chairman.

He told Nellie when he signed the tariff bill that he fully expected "to be damned heartily in many corners of the Capitol and elsewhere," but he believed he had done what was right "and that must be my solace." There was little other solace for Taft. Words of praise were few. While he could claim he had halted the upward tide, he had brought about no sweeping reductions and on thousands of items tariffs remained at the same level as under the old laws. A dissatisfied and angry public, led to hope that prices of almost everything would go down when Taft revised the tariff, found that most things cost what they always had.

Some of the newspaper attacks against him were provoked less by editorial opinion than by the anger of newspaper business offices. There had been little reduction in the tariff on newsprint, which vitally affected the earnings of the largest newspapers. His poor press relations became even worse when he asked Congress to increase second-class postal rates on newspapers and magazines. Whether for business reasons or because of honest opinion, the editorial fury rose. Cartoonists pictured him as the deceiver of haggard women carrying empty market baskets, and the *New York World* called him a man who was against the people and for "privilege, plutocracy and betrayal of the party faith." He became the chosen villain of Democrats, Republican insurgents, and of Roosevelt men who accused him of being a "Presidential weakling" for not clubbing down Congress as they were convinced Roosevelt would have if we were still President. But Roosevelt, at the time, wrote from the African jungle that he thought the tariff had "come out as well as we could hope."

In the midst of the tariff furor, there came a personal shock that made Taft's political worries small for a time. Nellie, planning to take a brief trip with Taft and an official party down the Potomac to Mount Vernon aboard the Presidential yacht, and greatly upset for weeks by the abuse heaped upon her husband, suffered what apparently was a cerebral hemorrhage. The yacht had barely left the dock when she had what Taft later wrote his son, Robert, was "a very severe nervous attack, in which . . . she lost all muscular control of her right arm and her right leg and of the vocal cords and the muscles governing her speech." She was carried to a cabin while the yacht was turned back to dock and then she was rushed to the White House.

Doctors first feared brain paralysis and the night of waiting for some more hopeful diagnosis was unbearable for Taft. "The President looked like a great stricken animal," his aide, Archie Butt, wrote. "I have never seen greater suffering or pain on a man's face."

Nellie gradually recovered, but her speech was affected for a long time. Taft took her to a cottage at Beverly, Massachusetts, to recuperate. There, as Nellie's health improved, he found comfort in the fact that in being away from Washington she seemed to be less "bothered by the storm of abuse to which I have been subjected."

By late August, 1909, he was able to find some relaxation himself at nearby golf links and by taking "swift motor car rides," and had decided to present "a clear statement of facts" directly to the people of the nation by making a speaking tour of the country. He was sure he could clear away all the hostility if the people only could be made to understand.

He set out in September on a 13,000-mile swing to the West Coast and back, during which he would deliver 259 speeches in less than three months as a Presidential traveling salesman of good will and calm reasoning. Taft had no speech writers or press secretaries skilled in the delicate task of handling of public opinion. Most of his speeches were made up on the spot, or hurriedly dictated between whistle stops, platform appearances, civic celebrations, cornerstone layings, parades, fairgrounds visits and political handshakings, with correspondents aboard the special Presidential train and local reporters wherever he went ready to make what headlines they could of any slip of his tongue. At every stop, there would be sensitive political and local situations to handle, long-winded oratory to suffer through, banquets at which he would be over-stuffed and hurried days when he would be underfed.

The trip was a circus all the way with what Taft described as "curiosity to see the President" as its main attraction. Flashlights exploded in his face, bands serenaded him at midnight, choruses of shrieking factory whistles blasted his sleep, flocks of fluttering pigeons were released to honor him, enormous maps of the United States flashed greetings in blinking colored lights, and he was even asked to don a bathing suit and pose in a hotel swimming pool to promote the benefits of warm spring baths, which was one indignity he refused. Wryly amused by the carnival atmosphere, he good-naturedly went along with most committee arrangements to exhibit him. But in the more serious purposes of his trip, he failed.

Most of his speeches, while sometimes rambling because they lacked advance preparation, were fair, honest and intelligent discussions of important problems of government. But his careful explanation asked more understanding than people aroused by the emotional attacks against him were willing to give. He won polite applause when he spoke of such things as the need for drastic reform of the American court system, but any mention of the tariff turned audiences to hostility. On that issue, the people seemed to have made up their minds from what they had read in the newspapers; the general feeling was that it was the worst tariff bill that had ever been perpetrated upon a suffering American public.

Taft's stop in the little town of Winona, Minnesota, had been planned so he could put in a few Presidential good words for James Tawney, chairman of the House Appropriations Committee, who was being criticized because he had voted for the tariff bill. For a month, Taft had been considering whether it might not be a good place to make his main speech in defense of the tariff, but he didn't get around to writing it until he was aboard the train approaching Winona. Between other stops, he dictated his thoughts to a stenographer and glanced through them only enough to straighten out the grammar.

He apologized to his audience at the Winona Opera House for the fact that the speech had been hastily prepared, but said he would read exactly what he had written because the subject called for "some care in expression." He pointed out that he had long advocated tariff reductions, told of his battles with the House and Senate, carefully analyzed various rate changes, and said neither he nor the Republican party had promised "to revise everything downward." He made no claim that the new law was perfect and clearly stated that it did not accomplish "certain things in the revision of the tariff which I had hoped for."

But it had been the first downward revision in the history of the Republican party, and the party for the first time had "conceded the necessity for . . . reducing tariff rates," so the bill was a "substantial achievement in the direction of lower tariffs," and it also contained provisions for more expert study of tariff problems in the future. Taft then spoke the one short sentence that was to be lifted out of his lengthy address, words that historians were to call perhaps the most self-damaging ever uttered by a President: "On the whole, therefore, I am bound to say that I think the bill is the best tariff bill that the Republican party ever passed."

Correspondents hurried to the telegraph office to file their stories. Headlines allowed no room for Taft's intelligent analysis of the faults and virtues of the bill. Newspapers across the country, in their boldest front-page type, proclaimed, with variations: TAFT CALLS TARIFF BEST IN HISTORY. Beneath the headlines, of course, were more complete versions of his speech, but it was the big black type that struck millions of Americans like a Presidential slap in the face.

Disgruntled farmers, laborers, office workers, housewives, read the headlines, thought of their mounting debts and the high prices they were paying for things, and were enraged. For weeks, the talk in country stores and over backyard fences was of what Taft had said, and the reaction was, "Who does he think he's trying to fool?" Editorialists, magazine writers, and political speakers picked up the words and echoed them into a roar. What more proof did anyone need, they asked in effect, than his own arrogant admission that he had gone back on his campaign promise and was in league with the bankers and the wicked profiteers?

Taft went on with his trip, and finally returned to Washington in November. But those words followed him all the way. Nothing he was later able to say or do changed the conclusion the public had jumped to, that President Taft had allied himself with the men of wealth and against the common people, and was actually boasting that he had put over "the best tariff in history."

** CHAPTER **

15

THEODORE ROOSEVELT returned to the United States on June 18, 1910, from his year of political self-exile in Africa, restless and ambitious for lost power. He was not yet ready to admit that he might change his mind about his promise never again to seek the Presidency. But the newspapers that had kept his name in headlines as the big game hunter who had slain 296 lions, elephants and water buffaloes in the African jungles already were predicting that his next safari would be a political hunt for the head of William Howard Taft.

His friendship with Taft, not yet broken, was badly strained. Gifford Pinchot, without waiting for Roosevelt's return, had gone to Europe to meet him and pour out a tale of woe. Other old friends had bombarded Roosevelt with letters to the effect that Taft was twisting all his policies and turning his back on Roosevelt men to align himself with reactionaries.

Taft meanwhile had come to the conclusion that many of Roosevelt's friends were his worst enemies and that the insurgents were out to ruin him and the Republican party. Taft also had sent friends to Europe, to appeal to Roosevelt to withhold decision until he personally learned all the facts. Just before Roosevelt sailed for home, Taft had sent him a letter explaining that he had been trying to carry out Roosevelt's policies, but "I have had a hard time" because the insurgents have "done all in their power to defeat us." He ended with a hearty invitation to Roosevelt to come stay as a guest at the White House so they could talk things over.

But Roosevelt, with cool formality, refused, saying he wanted to stay out of the political limelight for at least two months. He promised Taft that during that time he would make no political statements, and said, "I shall keep my mind open while I keep my mouth shut." Within a week, Roosevelt's home at Oyster Bay, Long Island, became a mecca for friendly reporters and for Taft's political enemies. By the end of the month, while still keeping his mouth shut about the Presidency, Roosevelt had actively reentered politics.

"I do not see how I am going to get out of having a fight with President Roosevelt," Taft told his aide, Archie Butt. "He seems to have thrown down the gauntlet. . . . I have doubted up to the present time whether he intended to fight my administration or not, but he sees no one but my enemies."

For the sake of party harmony a meeting finally was arranged between Taft and Roosevelt at the summer White House at Beverly, Massachusetts. Both men tried to carry it off with a show of cordiality, but they avoided any private discussion of their differences. Roosevelt jumped into the 1910 congressional election campaign with the announced intention of trying to bring the divided Republican party together, but instead of healing the break between liberals and conservatives, he greatly widened it. He refused to give the Taft administration his general endorsement and went into the Western states that were the homeland of the insurgents and campaigned for them in their rebellion against Taft and the regular party organization.

Taft was shocked when in his speeches Roosevelt attacked the courts as reactionary and described the whole judicial system as a fundamental barrier to social justice. In other speeches Roosevelt charged that state governments had failed to protect the rights of the people and called for extending the powers of the Federal government to regulate the social and industrial life of the nation.

Taft decided to "sit tight and let him talk," but in a letter to his brother, Charles, he accused Roosevelt of "going quite beyond anything that he advocated when he was in the White House," of acting as though "he considers himself still President," and of "hunting for reasons for criticizing me and justifying his attitude toward me." His "wild ideas," Taft said, "could never be gotten through without a revolution or revision of the Constitution."

A second Taft-Roosevelt meeting was arranged in September, 1910, at New Haven, where Taft was attending a session of the Yale Corporation, and this time they were closeted together for almost an hour. They came out afterwards smiling, but the meeting settled nothing between them. Taft commented privately that "if you were to remove Roosevelt's skull you would find written on his brain '1912.' "

Taft used his Presidential influence, patronage and party leadership to help conservative candidates fight insurgents, but his private prediction on election eve in November, 1910, was that there would be "a general Republican slump" because of the divided party. When the votes were counted, it was worse than a slump; it was a Republican disaster.

Democrats, for the first time in sixteen years, gained full control of the House of Representatives and enough seats in the Senate to throw the balance of power to the Republican insurgents who often voted with them. Key state elections for governors also were swept by Democrats. Among Republicans who lost was Warren G. Harding in Ohio, and among the newly elected Democratic governors was the former president of Princeton University, Woodrow Wilson of New Jersey. What was even more a blow to Taft's administration, almost the only Republican victories were in the West, where voters had elected insurgents.

But some of Roosevelt's favorite candidates also had lost;

Roosevelt soon decided any further effort to unite the two party factions was "pointless" and that he would make his open stand with the insurgents. Taft also had made a decision. Whether the Democrats went on to win the Presidency from him in 1912 or not, he was convinced that the Republican party and the nation would be best served in the long run by "sane" conservative views. At any cost, for the sake of its future, he believed the party would have to rid itself of "Roosevelt radicals."

Taft emerged from the disastrous 1910 election a more determined President and a more astute party leader. With greater political long-range planning than his enemies at first suspected, he systematically set about consolidating the remaining strength of the regular Republican party to capture full control for the conservatives and to build an organized machine that would be ready for 1912. As President, he worked with surer purpose to accomplish his own reforms by law so that before he finished his term he would be able to claim credit for a good many things that improved government and the public welfare.

Against the fierce opposition of bankers and their men in Congress, he established the Postal Savings Plan so that people in rural areas where there were few banks, and others with small funds, could deposit their money safely at any post office in low interest-bearing accounts. Over the strong protests of express companies who accused the government of direct competition with private business, Taft also signed into law a bill creating the parcel post service, giving Americans the right to mail packages as well as letters. During his administration the United States became a union of forty-eight states, with his signing of bills to admit New Mexico and Arizona.

Taft refused to go along with an attempt by Congress to keep immigrants from entering the United States unless they passed a literacy test proving their ability to read. He vetoed the bill on the grounds that if such a law had been in effect in previous years it would have barred many immigrants who had risen to importance and served their adopted country well. But his veto drew the wrath of leaders of organized labor, who feared an increasing flood of "illiterate foreigners" would lower wages of American workers. Labor also was offended when Taft named a woman to head a bureau of the Federal government for the first time in history, by putting Julia Lathrop in charge of the Children's Bureau he had created to deal with the then serious problems of child labor. In addition, he approved or created other labor agencies to help protect the health and safety of workers in mines and on railroads, and to extend coverage of workmen's compensation and employers' liability laws.

When the income tax that he had sent on its way toward ratification in the states met resistance, Taft urged support for it. He used his personal influence directly in Ohio by asking friends in the legislature to back the income tax resolution. Without income tax to finance it, most of the broad social legislation that came long after Taft's Presidency would have been impossible.

Taft put into effect the first important budgeting of government funds, after pointing out that "the United States is the only great nation whose government is operated without a budget." Until his time, the President had no direct supervision of government expenditures. Department heads went directly to Congress with estimates of funds they would need, with no unified planning or priorities. By executive order, Taft directed that all estimates must first come to him, so he could study requests and suggest where cuts could be made, and he got Congress to let him appoint a Commission on Efficiency and Economy "to find out exactly how the government of the United States is organized in each of its various branches." The commission became the forerunner of the national budget system, although it wasn't until 1920 that a Federal budget finally was established by law.

Having failed to win the tariff reforms he wanted, and with criticism of him still rising because of the tariff situation,

Taft tried an ambitious new approach to the problem—an attempt to cut duties by direct trade agreements with other countries. His hope was that by diplomatic negotiations he could get individual foreign nations and the United States to agree that each side would lower some of its tariff barriers on a reciprocal basis.

He started with Canada, whose popular Prime Minister, Sir Wilfred Laurier, was as eager as Taft to work out a common tariff plan which then would be put to a vote by each of their countries. After a long series of conferences between tariff experts on both sides, many of which included Taft himself, an agreement was reached to allow nearly all farm products and a number of other things to move duty free between both countries, and to lower rates on hundreds of other products. Taft carried the battle to Congress, refused to make compromises with special interests, fought down changes that might endanger the agreement, and finally brought the bill through both the House and Senate.

But the whole plan crashed to defeat, not because the United States rejected it, but because Canada did. During the Congressional debates in Washington, the new Democratic Speaker of the House, Champ Clark, in his enthusiasm for the Reciprocity Bill, declared: "I hope to see the day when the American flag will float over every square foot of the British North American possessions clear up to the North Pole." Others, including Taft himself, made some comments about greater cooperation between the two countries, and many Canadians, long in fear of American desires to annex Canada, became emotionally aroused over "threats" to take over their country and rose to the defense of their national honor.

Taft called the talk of annexation ridiculous and said it was just too silly to be taken seriously and should be treated as a joke. But it was no joke. Prime Minister Laurier staked his whole career on the issue, dissolved the Canadian parliament, and appealed to his people for a vote to approve the trade agreement. Laurier and Reciprocity were beaten, and so was Taft. The failure wasn't his, but after such renewed hopes of tariff reform the newspapers and the Roosevelt insurgents turned upon him with greater fury, charging that he was a bungler in everything, who sat idly in the White House while the nation went to ruin.

On another legislative front, Taft put real teeth into the old Interstate Commerce Act with railroad regulation bills he proposed, and which the insurgents in Congress rewrote to make even stronger. They gave the government substantial control over freight systems and railroad rate changes, and brought telephone, telegraph and cable companies under the supervision of the Interstate Commerce Commission.

Although President Roosevelt, with great publicity, had been the one to launch the government's war against the trusts and monopolies, Taft set a record of bringing twice as many court actions against them in his four years as Roosevelt had in seven years. Ever since he had helped revive the use of the then all but dead Sherman Antitrust Act by his ruling in the *Addystone Pipe Case* years before when he had been a circuit court judge, Taft had believed in the Sherman Act as an excellent legal weapon to save capitalism from its own excesses of corporate greed. He had chosen his "cabinet of lawyers" mainly to battle the trusts, and he put Attorney General Wickersham in direct charge of prosecutions. Taft's administration brought eighty-nine Sherman Antitrust actions, compared to Roosevelt's forty-three.

Taft wished again that he were on the Supreme Court himself instead of in the White House. "There is nothing I would have loved more than being Chief Justice of the United States," he said, when in 1910 he had to appoint a successor to Chief Justice Melville Fuller, who had died. "I cannot help seeing the irony of the fact that I, who desired that office so much, should now be signing the commission of another man." Another time, walking into the Capitol with his aide, Taft stopped to look up at a bronze statue of the great Chief Justice John Marshall, and was asked directly, "Would you rather have been him than President?" Taft answered quickly, "Of course. I would rather have been Marshall than any other American. . . . He made this country."

But he had one great satisfaction as President. He was able to appoint enough justices to pretty well make over the Supreme Court to his own liking. When Taft first became President, he confided to his old friend, Circuit Court Judge Horace Lurton, "The condition of the Supreme Court is pitiable." Chief Justice Fuller, he complained, was "almost senile," another justice "does no work," a third was "so deaf he cannot hear," two more "sleep almost through all the arguments." He wrote: "I do not know what can be done. It is most discouraging."

Within five months, Justice Rufus Peckham died, and Taft appointed Lurton, with whom he had served eight years on the circuit bench, to fill the vacancy. Soon Taft was predicting to his brother, Charles, that because of the infirmities of some of the remaining justices "I shall have the appointment of probably a majority of the Supreme Court before the end of my term." Early in 1910, Justice David Brewer died, and Taft named New York's Governor Charles Evans Hughes, with a half-promise that if the opportunity later came he might move Hughes up to Chief Justice.

But when Chief Justice Fuller did die only a short time later, Hughes did not become Chief Justice, a place he would not hold until years later when he finally succeeded Taft himself. At the time, anxious to choose a Chief Justice who would "coordinate the activities of the Court," Taft sent Attorney General Wickersham to sound out the justices themselves and to learn whom they wanted him to appoint. He was told the Court's first choice was one of its own members, Justice Edward White.

Taft was warned that he would be setting a "dangerous precedent" if he moved an associate justice to the center of the bench. He was also told that White would be about the most unpopular choice he could make as far as the voting public and his own Republican party were concerned. White happened to be a Democrat, a Roman Catholic, and a man who had fought on the Confederate side in the Civil War. Taft snapped that he wouldn't listen to "any talk of bigotry." He named Edward White Chief Justice, and was pleased when the nation's lawyers almost unanimously approved, newspapers praised his choice, and the Senate quickly confirmed it.

Before 1910 ended there was still another Court vacancy, and to fill that Taft chose Willis Van Devanter, a Cincinnati Law School graduate, former circuit judge and chief justice of the Wyoming Supreme Court, a man he knew to be a strict interpreter of the Constitution. Once again, in 1911, there was a Court opening. Taft's choice this time was the writer of Georgia's Code of Law, who had served that state's Supreme Court, Joseph Lamar. Taft's last chance to appoint a Supreme Court Justice came in 1912, and he named Chancellor of New Jersey Mahlon Pitney, who had been on New Jersey's Supreme Court.

Taft's prediction had been right. The men he chose constituted a majority of the Court. He had searched for those he considered the best experienced and had made a sincere effort to elevate the judicial quality of Presidential appointments to the Court he so greatly respected. But he also knew most of them would share his conservative views of government. The first duty of a Supreme Court Justice, Taft had said in 1910, was to "preserve the fundamental structure of our government as our fathers gave it to us."

✸✸ CHAPTER ✸✸

16

TAFT was the first President to have an official automobile and also the last to keep a cow to supply fresh milk for the White House table. Trying to meet the demands of an increasingly modern age, he was burdened by a small staff and the creaking machinery of an executive office that still required a President to give his personal attention to almost everything, so that he was frequently exhausted.

Many stories were told, some probably true, of his falling asleep while visitors were talking to him, of his sleeping through most of an official funeral, or snoring in his chair while a string ensemble played for guests at a White House musicale. Worry and overwork caused him to overeat, and his weight and girth spread to new dimensions despite his strenuous walks, medicine ball workouts, horseback rides, and frequent games of golf. Americans smiled over the newspaper pictures that showed four big workmen seated in the oversized bathtub installed in the White House to accommodate his bulk, and they loved such jokes as the one about his riding on a street car and politely getting up to offer three ladies his seat.

But the image of a lazy fat-man President ignored the fact that he managed to dig his way through mountains of detailed work while making delicate policy decisions, mediating government disputes, and traveling more miles to make more speeches and public appearances than any President in history. He appeared at fairs, state celebrations, college commencements, dedicated buildings and monuments, cut yards of ceremonial ribbons, and started a Presidential tradition by being the first to throw out a ball at the opening game of the baseball season.

As the more than honorary chairman of the Lincoln Memorial Commission, Taft chose the Potomac Park site, worked with architects, handled labor troubles, and finally got the work underway on building the Lincoln Monument after it had been stalled for more than forty years. Meanwhile Nellie encouraged the city of Tokyo to send the United States a good-will gift of several thousand young cherry trees. She had admired the trees while visiting Japan, wanted to beautify Washington by having them planted in the reclaimed park around the Tidal Basin, and so started the annual Cherry Blossom Festival.

There were few First Families more socially active than the Tafts. In addition to glittering formal receptions, there were almost nightly White House gatherings of some sort, dinners, card parties and dances. Some of Taft's daytime cat naps were due to the fact that he so enjoyed good company and so hated to see any party end that he seldom went to bed early enough to get a full night's sleep. He was still an excellent dancer and particularly enjoyed the young people's parties where he could display his talent not only as a master of the old-fashioned waltz but as a lively two-stepper who was right up to date when it came to dancing the "red wing" or the "grizzly bear."

"The greatest event in our four years at the White House" to Nellie was the celebration of their silver wedding anniversary in June, 1911, with an evening garden party that turned the White House lawn into a fairyland, with hundreds of colored lights and Japanese lanterns strung over the trees and shrubs. Like an American queen, wearing the diamond tiara that had been Taft's gift, she stood beside him to welcome nearly four thousand guests. The dining room inside was bannered with silken stars and stripes, and in the center was a towering anniversary cake, embedded with crystal hearts, girdled with roses and turtledoves, and decorated with cherubs rising from the scrolls of a frosted pastry sea. At midnight, Nellie retired, but Taft kept the party going until after two in the morning.

There wasn't much else that was fun for Taft that summer of 1911. He and Theodore Roosevelt had declared all-out political war. Roosevelt was still insisting that he would not be a candidate himself for the 1912 election, but he had encouraged Wisconsin's Senator Robert La Follette to form the National Republican Progressive League and to run against Taft as its independent candidate. Taft began a tour in early September that carried him thirteen thousand miles through twenty states in seven weeks to deliver 330 speeches. Announced as a non-political trip to "feel out the pulse of the nation," it actually was the start of his campaign for renomination. While he was busy making public speeches, his chief political organizer, Charles Dewey Hilles, was talking in every state to influential politicians. Hilles talked patronage and strategy, appointed Taft managers, lined up pledges, and won promised backing. He carefully sounded out the areas where Taft had the strongest potential delegate power and suggested what had to be done to mobilize the old guard party members to crush the insurgents. Back in Washington after the tour was over, almost daily conferences in the White House worked toward the goal of putting Taft men on the party's vital state committees and on the Republican National Committee.

When the Republican National Committee met in Washington on December 11, 1911, it finished its business in one day, deciding in Taft's favor on all issues before it. In quick order, the committee voted down attempts to reduce his delegate strength, and appointed pro-Taft subcommittees to organize the national convention that would meet in Chicago on June 18, 1912. Taft had every reason to be optimistic that he would win easy renomination in June. With the La Follette boom already dying, the Progressives had no real candidate. But Roosevelt, despite his continuing statements that he would not be a candidate, was a worry that haunted Taft.

On February 2, 1912, La Follette, exhausted by campaigning, suffered a temporary nervous collapse at a banquet in Philadelphia. That was the chance Roosevelt had been waiting for. He had a group of Republican governors issue a call for him to become a candidate. As the pressure mounted for him to take La Follette's place, scores of waiting Roosevelt supporters joined in urging him to let his name be used as his "duty to the nation."

In Cleveland, on his way to make a campaign-launching speech in Columbus, Roosevelt issued his battle cry: "My hat is in the ring. The fight is on and I am stripped to the buff!" Two weeks later, he formally announced his candidacy: "I will accept the nomination for President if it is tendered to me, and I will adhere to this decision until the convention has expressed its preference."

When the news reached the White House, Nellie said, "I told you so four years ago and you would not believe me." Although Taft was in no mood for laughter, her reaction made him laugh. "I know you did, my dear," he answered, "and I think you are perfectly happy now. You would have preferred him to come out against me than to have been wrong yourself."

Roosevelt, in his Columbus speech on February 12, struck directly at Taft's faith in the law to solve the nation's problems. He advocated more direct government by the people through judicial recall, initiative and referendum. When "a judge decides a constitutional question, when he decides what the people as a whole can or cannot do," Roosevelt said, "the people should have the right to recall that decision if they think it is wrong."

Taft answered in a speech in New York that there were "political emotionalists or neurotics" who were so eager for reform they were willing to "pull down those things which we have regarded as the pillars of the temple of freedom and representative government." He warned that such changes "would hurry us into a condition which could find no parallel except in the French Revolution or in bubbling anarchy."

Roosevelt returned the thrust and accused Taft of suffering from "political paranoia" for conjuring up visions of revolution. Taft had insisted he would carry on his campaign without "personal abuse," but the issues soon were lost in vitriolic name-calling from both sides. Roosevelt charged that Taft as President had betrayed him and his policies, and Taft felt he was the one who had been betrayed by Roosevelt's ambition to take back the Presidency. La Follette's loyal personal followers meanwhile tried to rally their forces against both Roosevelt and Taft to make a three-way fight for the Republican nomination.

To Taft, the battle to win renomination became far more important than whether he was reelected President. He had no great desire to serve another four years in the White House, but he was more than ever determined to rid the Republican party of the Roosevelt-La Follette influence, to drive out the insurgents and "radicals," and form the party around a solid conservative core for the future.

If he won renomination, he noted, "even though I were to go down to defeat," he would be able to "rally the conservative forces of this country and keep them in a nucleus of party strength, so that after four years the party could gather itself together and probably reestablish itself in control." He told friends, "My chief purpose in staying in is to defeat Mr. Roosevelt." Even if he were to be replaced in the White House by a Democrat, Taft felt, that would be less a permanent disaster than to let Roosevelt capture the Republican party.

Taft's national campaign, building for months with busy publicity men and speakers' bureaus, was supported in each state by the local old guard politicians who had smooth-running political organizations. Roosevelt's basic strategy, far more improvised and less well organized, was to present himself as the popular choice of the party's rank and file while he branded Taft the machine candidate of the bosses. Everywhere possible, the Roosevelt men called rump conventions to choose delegates of their own who would challenge the regularly chosen Taft delegates for seats at the coming national convention. They also called for open primary elections, but in the first two primaries that were held Roosevelt was defeated. Then the Roosevelt tide began to turn.

Taft lost the primary in his own home state of Ohio. As the other contests rolled on, Roosevelt was victorious in every state primary except two, and in some states he defeated Taft by overwhelming votes. He could claim with some truth that he was the people's choice, but Taft still remained the party's choice. Where delegates had been chosen by the traditional state party conventions, instead of by primary election, Taft had triumphed. He had come through the campaign with a majority of pledged delegates.

Roosevelt charged that 254 of Taft's delegates had been chosen by fraud, a wild claim that he didn't expect to stand up. But he did hope that if he could get seats for some eighty of his claimed delegates he might at least block Taft's almost sure nomination on the first ballot. Two weeks before the convention opened in Chicago's Coliseum, the Republican National Committee began hearings, and it soon became obvious that the committee favored Taft. When the hearings ended after furious debates, 235 of the contested delegate seats were awarded to Taft and only nineteen to Roosevelt. Probably Roosevelt had a right to about thirty more, which still would not have given him a majority, but with those he might have had a chance to add enough delegates pledged to minor candidates so as to dictate the organization of the convention.

To Roosevelt, it was "political brigandage," and he did not

intend to sit still for it. He would lead the battle in Chicago himself, he said, to war against "the rascality of the Taft men." Decked out in a brand new Rough Rider's hat, he stormed into the Windy City with a promise to carry the fight for delegates to the floor of the convention. "It is a fight against theft," he shouted from his hotel balcony to a crowd of admirers massed below, "and the thieves will not win!"

"Soak 'em, Teddy!" the mob yelled back. A band struck up the song associated with his days of Spanish-American War glory, "There'll Be a Hot Time in the Old Town Tonight," and when he grinned and lifted his fist, the responding cheer was deafening. Back in his hotel room, reporters asked him how he felt about his chances. With another wide grin, Roosevelt told them, "I'm feeling like a bull moose!"

On the eve of the convention, twenty thousand people crowded into a nearby auditorium where Roosevelt was to speak. Aroused by what to many had become a religious crusade against "political wickedness," they sang, "Onward, Christian Soldiers." Roosevelt told them: "We fight in honorable fashion for the good of mankind; fearless of the future; unheeding of our individual fates; with unflinching hearts and undimmed eyes; we stand at Armageddon, and we battle for the Lord!"

In Washington, where Taft remained at the White House during the Chicago convention, receiving reports by phone, he told friends, "It is possible that by bulldozing . . . he may reduce my vote . . . but I very much doubt that he can nominate himself as long as I stay in the field, and I shall stay as long as my remaining will defeat Roosevelt's purpose."

The Roosevelt fight was all but lost in the first hours after the convention began, when the Taft forces held firm and elected Elihu Root as chairman. Roosevelt lost his bid to control the convention by only fifty-seven out of more than one thousand votes, but when Root took command the convention battle, for all practical purposes, was already over. With Root in the chair delegate disputes would be ruled in

Taft's favor, the convention would be tightly run under Taft control, and it was a foregone conclusion that Taft would be nominated.

The convention's second day saw emotional bedlam as delegate rulings officially went against Roosevelt and his supporters set up a rhythmic chant, "We want Teddy! We want Teddy!" There were fist fights, people mounted desks to make impromptu speeches on the convention floor, and a flag-waving march through the aisles lasted nearly an hour before Root brought the convention to order and started to put through Taft motions as fast as he could tap his gavel. Roosevelt, in the face of continued rulings against him, sent word to his delegates to sit tight and refuse to vote.

Most of the Roosevelt delegates sat in silent protest, refusing to take any part in the proceedings on the last day of the convention, when to nobody's surprise Taft was renominated. Ohioan Warren G. Harding made the nominating speech, and after four days of wrangling, the convention made Taft its choice in two hours. Taft's total of 561 votes was almost exactly what he had estimated before the convention began. Taft had kept the party machine in his hands and it had nominated him. He had kept Roosevelt from taking over the Republican party.

Roosevelt's delegates, including those who had been refused convention seats, stormed out to a meeting in nearby Orchestra Hall and among themselves independently nominated Theodore Roosevelt for President. Roosevelt answered their call with a speech he began, "Thou shalt not steal . . ." He agreed to run as a third party candidate if a new party was formed and he was nominated by its convention. The convention was held in Chicago in August and the Progressive party of 1912 was born, with a platform drafted by Roosevelt, who was nominated by acclamation. Because of the remark he had made about feeling like "a bull moose," most Americans called it the Bull Moose party.

He had broken the Republican party, torn it wide open,

but he also had carried himself and his followers out of it. The conservatives were in command. By defeating Roosevelt for the nomination and by holding the old guard forces in line for the future, Taft had achieved his main objective, even if the party had been made smaller and might be politically weaker for a time.

Meanwhile the Democrats, who could hardly lose the coming election against the divided Republicans, went through a mighty scramble at their own June convention in Baltimore, and after forty-six ballots nominated New Jersey's reform governor, Woodrow Wilson. Under the circumstances, Taft had no illusions at all that he himself might win a second term. Publicly he went through the motions of the Presidential campaign, but it was all something of an anticlimax. He had achieved his own victory in Chicago by blocking Roosevelt's nomination. The Presidential years had been the unhappiest of his life and he looked forward to an escape from them.

He went home to Cincinnati to vote on election day and to wait out the returns, but he didn't have long to wait. The result was clear within a few hours. The divided Republican vote had swept Wilson into office. Together, Roosevelt and Taft had nearly one and one-half million more votes than Wilson, a Republican total almost unchanged from 1908, but the Republican vote was split and the Democratic vote united. On the basis of electoral votes, Taft's was the worst disaster ever suffered by the candidate of a major party. He carried only two states, Utah and Vermont, for a pathetic total of eight electoral votes.

"What I got," Taft said, "was the irreducible minimum of the Republican party after Roosevelt got through with it." In a New York speech shortly after the election, Taft asked his audience to join him in a toast: "Health and success to the able, distinguished, and patriotic gentleman who is to be the next President of the United States!"

He still had to wait out the months from November to

March before Wilson took over and he could quit the White House. "The nearer I get to the inauguration of my successor," he wrote, "the greater the relief I feel." When disappointed supporters suggested that he might stage a comeback and run for President again in four years, Taft said it was not even a possibility. "I have proven to be a burdensome leader and not one that aroused the multitude," he wrote candidly. "I am entirely content to serve in the ranks."

In an exchange of friendly letters with incoming President Wilson about White House living arrangements, Taft wrote that the salary and expense account more than covered most things and that "I have been able to save from my four years about $100,000." He told Wilson he was "looking forward to the fourth of March with feelings of contentment and satisfaction." First, there would be a month of "rest and golf at Augusta," and then he would be returning to Yale, where he had agreed to become a professor of law.

March 4, 1913, came at last. When President Wilson finished his inaugural address, Taft warmly congratulated him. "I wish you a successful administration," he said, "and the carrying out of your aims. We will all be behind you." He rode back to the White House with Wilson, stayed for lunch with him, and then he and Nellie boarded the train for Augusta and retirement to private life. He felt "a sense of freedom that I have never had before," and humorously observed, "Being a dead politician, I have become a statesman."

** CHAPTER **

17

PARADING Yale students, with cheerleaders and bands, escorted Taft to the university on April 1, 1913, while the people of New Haven crowded the streets to welcome the former President. He made a brief speech about finding himself out of work when he left the White House and jokingly said that "when I took inventory all I had was a somewhat tarnished reputation as a lawyer, a profession that I had abandoned thirty years ago."

He was returning to Yale "with no great claim to erudition," he said, "but with the earnest hope that from a somewhat extensive and varied experience I may have gleaned something which may be of use to the young men with whom I shall come in contact." He fully expected to become "a permanent resident of New Haven," and soon contentedly told friends, "I expect to live and die a professor."

He held two active professorships and taught two types of classes at the same time. As Kent Professor of Law in Yale College, his purpose was to give general students who elected his course a broader cultural understanding of the Constitution and processes of government. He also was professor of constitutional law at Yale Law School, where his course was required for students who expected to become lawyers.

Because Taft felt it wasn't right for him to be on the board at the same time he was on the faculty, he resigned from the controlling Yale Corporation, of which he had been a member since 1906. He insisted upon being put on an equal footing with the rest of the faculty, with whom he established an informal, first-name relationship. He regularly attended faculty meetings as a working member and actively helped to develop curriculum changes, revised entrance examinations, new courses and a strengthened teaching staff.

But at first, Taft was a disappointingly dull teacher. His college classes were large for those years, with as many as 120 students, and he tried to teach by the recitation method, keeping closely to the textbook and making few comments of his own. As the novelty of having a former President as a teacher wore off, the students became bored, so much so that some of them started making cash bets in the back of the room against the odds of having to recite on any given day. His course became so humdrum that if he were a few minutes late arriving he would find the students gladly had taken the excuse to walk out.

Finally a small group of more serious students went to his office to protest that they were just wasting their time. Taft took it well, admitted that the classes had been going badly, and asked for their suggestions. They suggested that instead of having class members recite, he should lecture himself, and follow each lecture with a brief written quiz. He agreed to try it and his classes soon became so interesting and inspiring that students sometimes rose to applaud him. He all but forgot the textbook and talked freely out of his own experience.

He told about judges who had written certain decisions, illustrated historic principles with firsthand information about bills he had signed or vetoed, told about his part in cases that went to the Supreme Court. His lectures were filled with jokes, anecdotes and vivid personal recollections, and he began to enjoy the informality of the classroom situation. His students, in turn, were able to enjoy the fresh insights he gave them of government at work and of the law as dramatic and human rather than dry text. In the law school, his classes were much smaller, with sometimes only a dozen students, and for Yale's future lawyers they became frank and revealing conversations with a former President about problems and people he had known.

Campus life delighted him. He was an enthusiastic follower of sports events, a debating team coach, leader of fund drives, speaker at fraternity dinners and other student affairs, and when he went to proms it was as a dancer, not a stand-off faculty member. He often took the side of students to help members of his classes settle difficulties with the faculty, supported a move to relax the rule prohibiting undergraduate marriages, and although he strongly criticized alumni who drank too much at reunions, he was inclined to be lenient with students who occasionally had a few drinks too many.

When he discovered students cheating, instead of preaching to them on moral grounds, he tried to make them realize they were cheating themselves of the education they had paid for and had gone to a lot of trouble to get. Cheating, he believed, simply marked a man as less intelligent than others, one who was too stupid to achieve things on his own ability. "When you get to be as old as I am," he said, "you will have observed that a man who cheats generally does so because he needs to."

New Haven's residents, like those on campus, soon became accustomed to having a celebrity in their midst, and he was able to stroll about the streets without attracting crowds. He enjoyed the freedom of walking alone, visiting shops, going to the tailor's with a pair of pants that needed pressing slung over his arm. But some townspeople still were surprised when the former President turned up among "soap box" orators at a street corner rally for civic improvement.

He was officially sworn in as a registered voter and citizen of New Haven at City Hall on October 24, 1914, along with a group of other "new voters," and like the rest was required to take a literacy test by reading part of the Constitution aloud. When he finished, he turned to the crowd and joked that now he had proof that "I really can read." He led city conservation movements, tree-planting drives, worked actively for the city planning commission to preserve parks and end unsightly urban sprawl, and took a special interest in New Haven's foreign-born residents.

Taft spoke frequently to service clubs and community meetings on the need for tolerance for all racial and religious groups and his liberal religious views made him a popular speaker for Catholic, Protestant and Jewish organizations. He helped administer and manage the national affairs of his own faith as president of the American Unitarian Association and later head of the Unitarian General Conference.

His salary of $5,000 a year as a Yale professor was quite a drop from the $100,000 in salary and expenses he had been paid as President, but requests came in from all over the country for him to speak and as organizations started bidding for his services lecturing became his main source of income. His secretary, Wendell Mischler, who had been with Taft since he was Secretary of War, turned his four-room suite of offices in the Hotel Taft into what amounted to a one-man lecture bureau and Taft became one of the busiest public speakers in the United States. Mischler was busy until midnight nearly every night booking engagements with civic groups, colleges and universities, women's clubs, chambers of commerce, manufacturers' associations, conventions, lyceums, and along the Chautauqua circuit. Taft's lecture fee averaged $400 and sometimes ran to $1,000 or more. He also was highly paid for articles he wrote for popular magazines such as *The Saturday Evening Post*.

Taft had come to Yale with the understanding that he would be given as much free time as possible to devote to public affairs and his class schedules were arranged so that he was able to be away from New Haven three or four days a week on speaking trips. During college and summer vacations, his tours were more extended. Often he spoke at several different places the same day. Mischler found that he could book Taft for a Saturday night speech as far away as Iowa and still allow him to catch a midnight train that would bring him back to New Haven in time to hold a regular Monday morning class. When he was asked about the secret of successful speaking, Taft laughed and said, "I always consider any speech to be successful if more of my audience stay than leave during the course of the speech."

Lecturing became so profitable that Taft noted in 1915 that if he could keep up the schedule for another three or four years he would put enough money into the bank to ensure an income of $10,000 a year for the rest of his life. His paid lectures also helped finance the travels that let him speak without a fee to charitable organizations, and to address state legislatures and bar association groups. He had become president of the American Bar Association in 1913.

He and Mischler drew up a list of about thirty subjects on which he was prepared to lecture and the list was sent to any organization that invited Taft to speak so that it could choose its own topic. Taft was busy preparing new speeches suggested by current events, but he also had a number of "standard" addresses that he used many times with minor variations. Sometimes he spoke extemporaneously or from only an outline, but more often he read from a tried and true typewritten text. The total number of public appearances he made reached into the thousands. In nearly all his speeches, whatever the subject, he stressed the theme of sound, conservative constitutional government.

Taft wrote all his talks and articles himself with no research assistants to help prepare them. When he got an idea for a new speech, he would dictate his thoughts to Mischler, then go to the Yale library to dig out supporting facts or quotations, and work rapidly to prepare the final version after one or two drafts. Aboard a train on his way to deliver one speech, he frequently would revise another, or would finish up some article he had agreed to write for a magazine.

Despite the punishing amount of work he did and the schedule that kept him hopscotching about the country between classes as a professor, he seldom appeared overworked, and to his friends he still seemed as unhurried and easygoing as ever. He never missed a deadline or speaking engagement, although he once complained that he was booked on the same night in places so far apart that "only a bird" could get from one to the other fast enough "and I haven't many bird-like qualities."

Politically, as the nominal leader of the Republican party, he confined his leadership to active work within the party in opposition to the Democrats and President Wilson, but made it definite that his own days of office-seeking were finished. As 1916 approached, he was among those who decided that Charles Evans Hughes would make the party's best candidate. Hughes had little desire to resign from the Supreme Court to run for President, but Taft was greatly responsible for getting him to change his mind. He helped plan the party strategy that would make Hughes the obvious choice of the Republican National Convention, so that Hughes could hardly refuse the call, and then used his personal influence to get Hughes to take the nomination.

Taft stayed away from the convention in Philadelphia, but kept in close touch by telephone. When Hughes was nominated as planned, he was delighted and certain at first that "we are going to rally to victory." He promised Hughes his active support, and made one long campaign tour for him in October and other shorter speaking trips. But by election eve, Taft was depressed and told Nellie he had "an uneasy feeling that we may be facing a landslide for Wilson."

When the returns were counted, it was no great landslide, but Hughes was defeated and Wilson reelected, and to Taft it was a "bitter cup to swallow." He was particularly concerned because "poor Hughes is lifted out of the Supreme Court." But when Taft sent him his consolations, Hughes replied, "You must not chide yourself for urging me to make the fight. . . . I did not wish to leave the bench, but it was a high privilege to be chosen to lead . . . I have no complaints and no regrets."

During the Hughes campaign, Taft and Roosevelt began to bridge their enmity. Their first meeting after battling for the Presidency was at funeral services in New Haven for Yale Professor Thomas Lounsbury on April 13, 1915, when both were asked to act as honorary pallbearers for their mutual friend. They managed to smile, exchange formal greetings, ask about each other's health, and then to ignore each other for the remainder of the service.

By 1916, Roosevelt was back in the Republican party and supporting Hughes, as Taft was, and campaign leaders finally arranged for them to share the same speaking platform at a reception for Hughes in New York. Taft and Roosevelt shook hands and then went into the meeting room to deliver separate speeches. Afterwards, for the benefit of reporters, they shook hands again, and turned to walk off in opposite directions. But in the months that followed they exchanged a few polite letters, and both agreed with friends that they should make up, but neither seemed willing to take the first step toward a real reconciliation.

Their next meeting was by accident. Taft happened to be in Chicago early in May, 1918, stopping at the Blackstone Hotel, and on his way up in the elevator he learned that Roosevelt was dining at the hotel. Impulsively, Taft took the elevator back down, walked into the dining room, and crossed to the table where Roosevelt was seated alone.

Other guests, already somewhat agog over the fact that Roosevelt was among them, recognized Taft and a hush came over the dining room. Taft said, "Hello, Theodore." Roosevelt looked up, surprised, and then grinned and clasped the hand Taft held out to him. As they shook hands heartily, the other diners rose from their tables and cheered. Taft and Roosevelt sat together and talked for more than half an hour. "He was really much pleased," Taft noted, "and very cordial."

Much later, Taft wrote Roosevelt's sister, Mrs. William Cowles, to tell her how glad he was that "Theodore and I came together after that long painful interval."

Roosevelt was not well. He had partially lost his hearing, was blind in one eye, and was suffering from a blood infection. It was to be their last meeting. Nine months later, on January 5, 1919, Roosevelt died. Taft went to his funeral in New York, accompanied the family to the grave, and at memorial services later said, "How much we have lost in him grows upon us. . . . He spoke to and moved the common man . . ."

** CHAPTER **

18

TAFT was vacationing at Murray Bay in the summer of 1914 when war came to Europe and at first he found it hard to believe the news dispatches were true. Never had the prospects for international peace seemed more hopeful. It was incredible that Austria had declared war against Serbia at a time "when all good people had been hoping that the sentiment in favor of peace was growing."

He had been working for world peace for nearly twenty years. Back when he was still a circuit court judge, he had helped form the National Arbitration Committee. He had backed the efforts of Presidents Cleveland, McKinley and Roosevelt to bring about international peace agreements, and his own greatest regret as President had been the failure of his attempts to banish war with arbitration that would have real meaning. Taft had gone far beyond any previous President in nearly achieving agreements to arbitrate "questions of national honor," which were left out of most treaties.

"If we do not have arbitration, we shall have war," Taft warned in 1910 when he became honorary head of the American Society for the Judicial Settlement of International Disputes. Woodrow Wilson, then president of Princeton, had joined him in endorsing the aims of the group.

As President, Taft had worked out draft agreements with Britain and France for the settlement of disputes by an international court of arbitration, and had hopefully looked forward to pacts with other nations, arguing that America must agree to include the vital questions of national honor that "when they arise are likely to lead to war." Taft's efforts had encouraged industrialist Andrew Carnegie to give ten million dollars of his fortune to create the Carnegie Peace Fund. "It is based on your words," the steel magnate had written Taft. But in the end, Taft's treaties and his plan for meaningful international arbitration had been killed by the Senate. When he left the White House, he had said, "We must hope and work on." He had worked on, while he was a professor at Yale, and popular support for peace movements had been growing, both in the United States and in Europe.

And now, incredibly, in the summer of 1914, there was war in Europe. When the news was confirmed, Taft issued a statement to the press: "All we can do now is hope that those responsible for the foreign policy of Russia and Germany will localize the trouble, so that we shall not have a general European War." But almost as he spoke, the war spread. Russia mobilized. Germany's Kaiser, fearing the alliance between Russia and France, struck suddenly at France through Belgium. England declared war on Germany.

When President Wilson called for strict American neutrality, declaring that the United States must be "neutral in fact as well as in name," Taft prayerfully agreed. But Wilson soon found absolute neutrality impossible to preserve. The British navy blockaded Germany and stopped American trade with much of Europe. American vessels, some of which were carrying goods to Germany, were illegally searched and seized by the British. Germany, in January, 1915, struck back at the English blockade by proclaiming and carrying out submarine warfare in a wide zone around the British Isles, and the U-boat menace threatened the lives of American merchant sailors as well as American profits.

As the man Wilson had defeated for the Presidency, as the leader of the opposition party, Taft was and would remain Wilson's political foe. But as a man of peace, he was determined to uphold the President, even against other leaders of his own party. Belgium had been occupied and the clamor by many Americans to enter the war on the side of England and France grew louder, but in a speech at Morristown, New Jersey, late in February, 1915, Taft called for national unity in support of President Wilson. "We must abide by the judgment of those to whom we have entrusted the authority, and when the President shall act, we must stand by him to the end," he said. "All will forget their differences in self-sacrificing loyalty to our common flag and our common country."

A clipping of Taft's speech was put on Wilson's desk and the President commented, "This is certainly fine and generous." Republican Senator Henry Cabot Lodge, who was told about Wilson's reaction, remarked sourly that it was all "too damned fine and generous," but Taft's stand was hailed by others as "making the administration's policy an American policy."

When a German submarine sank the British luxury liner *Lusitania* off the coast of Ireland on its way to New York on May 7, 1915, there were 128 Americans among those lost in the sinking, and the nation braced itself for a possible declaration of war. But President Wilson, still trying desperately to remain neutral, declared, "There is such a thing as a nation being so right that it does not need to convince others by force. . . . There is such a thing as a man being too proud to fight."

Taft, who had said almost the same thing in advocating his peace treaties when he was President, heartily approved. "I sincerely hope that President Wilson will save us from war," Taft wrote. "I have been President, and I know what an awful responsibility a man has to carry in such a crisis . . . trying to find the right way."

He sent a long personal letter to Wilson "to express, in a

deeply sympathetic way, my appreciation of the difficult situation you face." Wilson's answer was warm and grateful. He said the whole nation admired, as he did, Taft's spirit in submerging party differences. Taft continued making speeches supporting Wilson's struggle for neutrality, while Roosevelt's followers denounced Wilson as a spokesman for "flapdoodle pacifists" who were "too yellow to fight." In a speech in Philadelphia, Taft said, "The task of the President is a heavy one. He is our President. He is acting for the whole country. He is anxious to find a way out of the present difficulty without war. Before party, before ourselves, we are for our country. That is what he is working for. . . . Let us stand by him in this juncture. Our honor is safe with him."

For months, Wilson went on exchanging diplomatic notes with Germany, but all mediation attempts finally failed. In February, 1917, Germany resumed unrestricted submarine warfare. For two years, the United States had stayed out of "Europe's War," but now diplomatic relations were broken, American merchant ships were armed, and three of them were sunk by German submarines. War had come and Wilson went before Congress on April 2 to ask for its declaration. Germany's war, he said, was "warfare against mankind . . . a war against all nations," and although it was "a fearful thing to lead this great peaceful people into war," the "right is more precious than peace" and the "world must be made safe for democracy."

Taft threw himself into the work of "winning the war." He became one of the most successful speakers of the Liberty Loan drive, traveling eight thousand miles during one two-month tour. There were times when he became caustically critical of President Wilson's management of the war. But when the President asked him to help reduce labor troubles that were endangering production in vital war industries, Taft immediately agreed to serve the administration.

By the fall of 1917, factory strikes and lockouts were seriously interfering. Some employers had refused to meet the sharply increased wartime costs of living with adequate wages. Labor troubles were spreading. The Council of National Defense called for a conference among employers and labor leaders to find out, as Taft put it, "whether we can arrange a truce between labor and capital in this country." A War Labor Conference Board was created, with five employer members and five labor representatives, and Taft was named to head it as cochairman, along with a liberal Missouri attorney who had been prominent in industrial relations work, Frank P. Walsh.

Taft at first considered Walsh an "unsound radical," but before long decided he was a man to be admired, and although their basic economic views were far apart, they worked well together as cochairmen. Somewhat to his own surprise, Taft found himself siding with the labor leaders in many of their complaints and even having to "read the riot act" to employer representatives.

The conference drew up a statement of principles to be used in settling wartime labor disputes that were so liberal it brought "scandalized protests" from America's conservative business and industrial leaders. But Taft joined in writing and signing it, and gave it his full approval.

Employers were forbidden to discharge workers for union membership or activities, the right to unionize and bargain collectively was not to be "denied, abridged or interfered with by employers in any manner whatsoever," health and safety regulations were to be strictly enforced, and women doing men's work were to receive equal pay. Most revolutionary of all the conference terms was the setting up of a "living wage" as the basis for fixing pay schedules. All workers, the conference decided, were entitled to a living wage based on a minimum that would "insure the subsistence of the worker and his family in health and reasonable comfort."

The conference recommended the creation of a National War Labor Board. President Wilson appointed Taft and Walsh its cochairmen. Taft took a formal leave of absence from Yale on April 15, 1918, moved to Washington, and for more than a year put aside his professorship to work at settling labor disputes.

In all his years as judge, cabinet member, President and law professor, he had never been really close to the down-to-earth problems of workers. Heading the War Labor Board was a liberal experience. Instead of considering such things as minimum wages and the struggle to organize in abstract legal and economic terms, he was brought face to face with workers themselves and with those who led the factory-level fights for union recognition. His labor views remained conservative, but they were tempered with a new understanding.

Taft realized that he lacked practical experience in handling labor disputes, so instead of sitting at his desk in Washington he started his work with the War Labor Board by presiding in person at a series of hearings at various Southern textile mills and munitions factories. What he heard from the workers, and the conditions he saw, brought him back to Washington both exhausted and angry. He informed his fellow board members that he didn't see "how people can live on such wages." Taft issued an order, approved by the board, that tripled some of the wages that were in dispute.

He stood with the board against so-called "yellow-dog" contracts, hated by labor, whereby some companies hired workers only after they signed pledges not to unionize. In carrying out the board's policy of awarding a living wage to all workers, Taft often was impatient with company arguments that wage increases would force higher prices or drive manufacturers out of business. But at the same time, he insisted in other rulings on "being just and fair to capital."

Although the board had no legal authority to enforce its rulings, its decrees were backed by all the vast wartime emergency powers of the President. Companies or industries that refused to accept the board's mediation or its decisions often had their plants taken over by the War Department. Taft presided at dozens of hearings himself, read hundreds of documents and briefs, studied involved cases in detail, and took part in awards and findings that directly affected more than one thousand establishments with some 700,000 workers. Decisions made for one company frequently were adopted by an entire industry. The War Labor Board averted a total of 138 strikes, some of which would have disastrously affected war production.

Even greater in the long run was the influence it had upon the adoption of wage and hour standards, and on labor's continuing battle for fixed minimums and full union recognition. When armistice came, many employers cast aside the board's wartime rulings, but a precedent had been set for the tribunal that one day would pass on railroad labor disputes, and in years later for the National Labor Relations Board that came into being with President Franklin Roosevelt's New Deal.

With the war ending Taft had lost interest in the War Labor Board and was glad to leave Washington the last week in June, 1919, to return to Yale. He was already deeply involved in the "fight to win the peace," the battle he had never given up, to establish what now had become the hope for a League of Nations. By June, 1919, it was a battle already nearly lost.

** CHAPTER **

19

Two years before President Wilson publicly committed himself to his plan for a League of Nations, Taft began preaching the league idea. His version of a league was different from what Wilson's became, but many things he advocated were made part of it, and his work in educating public opinion greatly strengthened Wilson's role. Throughout the whole struggle for it, the League of Nations had no better friend than Taft.

Wilson's supreme goal from the beginning was a just peace upon which a new world order could be established and maintained through an international association. But Wilson was determined to keep control of the movement in his own hands, and while he waited for public support to grow his declared views were deliberately general and not specific. Taft took the leadership by backing a League to Enforce Peace, and became president of the non-partisan group of distinguished citizens who organized it at a conference on June 17, 1915, in Philadelphia's Independence Hall.

Broadly, the League to Enforce Peace was based on the theories Taft had tried to write into treaties while he was President, but what was new was that the plan called for international enforcement of peace. If any member nation of the proposed league went to war or committed acts of hostility, without first bringing its quarrel before an international court, then all nations were to join in using "both their economic and military forces" against the peace-breaking nation.

Taft explained in a speech that launched the project that the group was not trying to suggest ways to end the immediate war in Europe, that they had no official standing and represented nobody but themselves, but that they hoped to arouse public opinion that would influence world leaders to consider "a plan for an international agreement by which, when this present war shall cease, a recurrence of war will be made less possible. . . . We think a league could be formed which would enable nations to avoid war by furnishing a practical means of settling international quarrels, or suspending them until the heat of passion has cooled."

He stressed the need to include the doctrine of force "in any league that is to prove useful," and also foresaw the possibility that the league might become sort of an international legislature, holding regular congresses to amplify the principles of international law. "We have got to depart from the traditional policy of this country," he said. "We are so near to all the nations of the world today that we are vitally interested in keeping war down as far as we can. . . . We had better step forward and assume certain obligations in the interest of the world and in the interest of mankind, because there is a utilitarian reason for it—we are likely to be drawn in ourselves. . . . Therefore we ought to depart from the policy of isolation. . . . We must bear our share of the responsibilities and we must help along the world, and incidentally help along ourselves."

So began what was to be the great national debate over a proposed association of nations. Taft's announcement of the planned League to Enforce Peace brought immediate support, but also strong opposition. Within a year, the group had raised

$350,000 for propaganda purposes, and Taft devoted much of his time to it.

President Wilson favored the aims of the league and spoke at a dinner for it presided over by Taft, but for months he politely rebuffed Taft's attempts to get him to declare himself publicly for the league. Finally, on the eve of America's entry into the war, in his famous "Peace Without Victory" speech to the Senate on January 22, 1917, Wilson set forth the conditions upon which he would "feel justified in asking our people to approve its formal and solemn adherence to a league for peace." What the President had in mind was his own league, but he did back the idea of an enforced peace which was the keystone of Taft's league.

On January 8, 1918, as the war neared its end, President Wilson made his speech to Congress on war aims and peace terms in which he laid down the Fourteen Points he considered the "only possible" program for world peace to be negotiated in Paris. Last among them, but for Wilson a goal for which he eventually would sacrifice almost all the rest, was "a general association of nations . . . under specific covenants" for guaranteeing "political independence and territorial integrity" to all nations.

Wilson had decided by early 1918 that when the time came he would head the American delegation to the Paris peace conference himself. He also had made it clear to Taft that when details of a possible league of nations were drafted, he would draft them himself. When Taft's group announced plans for a convention in Philadelphia, the President called him to the White House and said that such a meeting might embarrass him in making his own plans.

Taft was discouraged by the President's attitude and was afraid he was ready to abandon the league idea. They had another luncheon conference which worried Taft even more when Wilson said the Senate would never consent to letting a majority of other nations tell the United States when it must go to war. Taft wrote afterwards that the President was "in one of his moods where he has now become opposed to the plan of the league," and that the force of public opinion was needed so that "he will come again to our view." Whether the President liked it or not, he decided to go ahead with the Philadelphia convention of the League to Enforce Peace.

Taft and Wilson soon came to a temporary parting of the ways for more political reasons. Anxious for a vote of confidence by the American people so that he could go to the Paris peace conference with what he hoped would be a mandate for his Fourteen Points, Wilson shattered the war-time political truce just before the Congressional elections in November, 1918, and turned the voting into a bitter partisan contest over his policies. He made a personal appeal to the nation, on the basis of patriotism, to vote against Republicans and elect a Democratic majority to Congress. Wilson's appeal was an affront to Taft and to many other Republicans who had loyally backed the war effort. Taft's old Roosevelt enemies, who had criticized him for his non-partisan stand, now said he had let Wilson make a fool of him.

Stung to the quick by the President's electioneering speech, Republicans turned out a vote that was a blow to Wilson's prestige. They captured both houses of the new Congress that would begin the following March. More tragic for Wilson's dream of peace was that the new Senate, from which he would have to win confirmation of the peace treaty, would have as the head of its powerful Foreign Relations Committee a Republican who was determined to cut Wilson's throat politically once and for all, Henry Cabot Lodge.

One week after the fateful 1918 election, the armistice that ended the World War was announced. Wilson's choice of the official delegation that would accompany him to the Paris conference did nothing to soothe Republican feelings. Instead of naming a bipartisan delegation that legitimately could claim to represent the national will, or that at least included some members of the Senate as was suggested, Wilson ignored both the Senate and the Republican leadership. He chose an official American Peace Commission that critics were quick to charge represented a just-defeated party in the United States.

Taft's son, Robert, was in Paris when the peace conference began at Versailles in January, 1919, and his first reports that "the President and the League of Nations are steadily losing ground," were discouraging. But Taft soon became convinced that Wilson was pressing hard for an effective League, and he did all he could to support him. He began a speaking tour that would carry him through fifteen states to urge all Americans to join him in letting the President know they were behind the League plan, and he pleaded that "it must not become a party question."

Wilson wrote from Paris to thank him, but Taft's Roosevelt foes and others harshly condemned him for supporting "Wilson's League." Taft dismissed them as "barking critics" whose partisan "selfishness and littleness" was "blinding them to the real interests of this nation as well as of the world." If Wilson brought back a "treaty worth having," nothing else mattered to Taft. "I don't like Wilson any better than you do," he told fellow Republicans, "but I think I can rise above my personal attitude in order to help along the world and the country. I don't care who gets credit for the League of Nations, if it goes through."

President Wilson took time out from the peace conference in February, 1919, after getting the first draft of the League of Nations covenant accepted as an integral part of the peace treaty, and came back to Washington to discuss possible changes. He was questioned at length by members of the Senate and House foreign relations committees, who met with him at the White House. Senator Lodge, as head of the Senate group, offered no changes at the meeting with Wilson. But a week later, Lodge issued a "round robin" statement, signed by thirty-seven Republican Senators, calling for rejection of the League "in the form now proposed."

On the same night that Senator Lodge issued his statement,

March 4, 1919, Taft and President Wilson stood arm in arm on the stage of the Metropolitan Opera House in New York, where both spoke to a vast gathering of League supporters. The League would be so interwoven with the peace treaty, President Wilson declared, that it could not be separated without "destroying the whole vital structure."

After Wilson returned to Paris, Taft wrote him that "senatorial opponents are speaking all over the country," and suggested some changes that might be made to satisfy the complainers. Wilson accepted his suggestions and three of Taft's recommendations were later written into the covenant almost in Taft's exact language, as well as a fourth one that Wilson simplified. Taft's revisions provided that a nation might withdraw from the League on two years' notice, that the League was not to consider purely domestic questions, that plans for limitations of armaments were to be revised every ten years, and that the League would specifically recognize the provisions of America's Monroe Doctrine.

But in Paris, Wilson found that England and France were demanding a conqueror's peace, and to preserve the League he was forced to give ground, little by little, on his Fourteen Points. The League finally became the one great thing he hoped to save as he was driven to sacrifice his other principles for compromises that would let him bring home any peace treaty at all.

Taft, like Wilson, could see only that the League, written into the final treaty, was to be a forceful safeguard against future wars. "The Republicans have been making fools of themselves," he noted, "by allowing their bitter personal opposition to Wilson to control their good sense. The people of this country are in favor of the League." Taft made another speaking tour. He arranged for conventions of League backers in fifteen major cities. By letter and in person, he appealed directly to Republican leaders and to Senators who would vote on ratification.

The Treaty of Versailles, completed late in May, 1919, and

signed a month later by the Germans who bitterly protested that it was a betrayal of the armistice they had accepted, was a travesty of the original war aims Americans said they had been fighting for, and millions of war-weary people around the world who had put their faith in the promises of democracy were disillusioned. Out of his Fourteen Points, Wilson really had salvaged only the League of Nations. But that had been approved and would be launched with every Allied signer of the Treaty of Versailles as a member, and he believed it would outweigh all he had lost.

Taft had prayed for some such hope of a world at peace. Everything would now depend upon what Wilson made of the opportunity to persuade the Senate to accept it. Whatever Taft thought of Wilson's "bungling" in Paris, he dared not lose faith that Wilson would make good this one great chance. He was sure that with so much at stake, Wilson would be "tactful and reasonable" in dealing with the Senate.

It was an exhausted President, fallen from his pinnacle as a world idol, who brought the treaty home and on July 10, 1919, submitted it to the Senate with a request for immediate ratification. But Senator Lodge and the Republicans who controlled the Foreign Relations Committee refused to be hurried. They spent weeks in hearings. Lodge did not attack the League directly, but proposed "to Americanize" the treaty by inserting amendments. Taft thought some modifications might be accepted to find a middle ground of compromise, so long as the changes were not the kind that would mean the treaty "will have to go back and receive the concurrence of the other Allied powers as well as that of Germany."

But Wilson would accept no change. He decided to carry his fight over the heads of the Senate and appeal directly to the people, and Taft was worried as Wilson began his cross-country speaking tour early in September. He knew from his own experience as President that such appeals could inflame opposition instead of quieting it. He hoped Wilson would discuss the League calmly and explain some of the things about it that troubled the nation.

Wilson was in no mood for explaining. Heartsick over the failures in Paris, desperate for this redeeming achievement of a League of Nations that could change the world, he demanded its acceptance. He warned that if the League were beaten or crippled by Senate amendments, "I can predict with absolute certainty that there will be another world war."

While he was away from Washington, the Foreign Relations Committee put the treaty before the Senate with fourteen reservations and amendments attached. Most of them drew few objections in the Senate. One, however, struck at what Wilson considered was vital to the League, the provision in Article Ten of the covenant which empowered the League Council to call member nations into combined action against any foreign aggressor. Lodge wanted it amended so that the United States would assume no such obligation without direct approval of Congress.

Wilson adamantly refused to consider it. He hated Lodge just as much as Lodge hated him and could be just as stubborn. He refused to accept any changes at all. Taft was greatly alarmed by the time Wilson had spoken his way across the country to the Pacific Coast. Wilson did not speak calmly. He attacked the League's enemies in the Senate by calling them names, by denouncing them as unpatriotic "bitterenders" and "irreconcilables." They were, he swore, "a battalion of death."

They also happened to be the men whose votes Wilson had to win in order to ratify his treaty. It seemed to Taft that by deliberately infuriating them, Wilson was destroying what chance there was to reason with them for Senate support. "Wilson is playing into their hands by his speeches in the West," Taft wrote. "It is impossible for him . . . to make speeches on the subject and explain the League without framing contemptuous phrases to characterize his opponents.

... The President's attitude in not consenting to any reservations at all is an impossible one."

At Pueblo, Colorado, on September 25, President Wilson collapsed under the strain after delivering his fortieth speech. Half-paralyzed by a stroke from which he never fully recovered, he was brought back to Washington. For seven months, he saw few visitors and received only the communications his wife allowed him to see. Cut off from knowledge of what was really happening in the Senate, he still sent commands from his sickbed to the Democrats in the Senate to fight for the treaty without amendment.

Taft hurried to Washington in late October as he realized the battle for the League was being lost. He pleaded with Senators, agreed with them that an amended treaty would be better than none at all, said that "even with reservations (it) represents enormous progress toward better conditions as to peace and war in the world." To get a League of Nations, he was even willing at last to agree to the reservations on Article Ten, which had been a basic principle of his own League to Enforce Peace. "I beg you," he told reluctant Senators, "consider the consequences if you defeat the treaty. . . . We are in sight of the promised land. Don't prevent our reaching there."

The Senate deadlocked over Article Ten. From the White House, Wilson sent one more imperious order to the Democrats. There was to be no compromise. The Senate must accept the League of Nations as he had planned it or accept nothing. Taft's feelings against both Lodge and Wilson turned to rage. He accused them of putting "their personal prestige and the saving of their ugly faces above the welfare of the country and the world."

On November 19, 1919, the Senate rejected the treaty. But there was an immediate demand for another vote to be taken in the next session of Congress. Taft clung to the hope "that the defeat of the treaty is not final" and that after the

Senators had listened to the people in their home states "they will come back with a willingness to put it through."

He was convinced it was Wilson's stubbornness that stood in the way. Taft's hatred for Wilson was such that he could hardly find the words to describe "that mulish enigma, that mountain of egotism and selfishness who lives in the White House." He had stood behind Wilson until it became obvious the Senate would never accept Article Ten. There was still this last chance to win ratification if Wilson would take the League with reservations.

But Wilson, who had made so many concessions at Paris, would make none to the Senate. The final vote came on March 19, 1920, and the treaty for a second time failed to get its two-thirds majority. It was sent back to the White House unapproved. Without the United States as a member, the shadow of a League of Nations would for years go through the motions of being a world organization for peace. But it would take another World War and another quarter of a century before America became part of a new United Nations' hope for peace, and even then with no granted power of real enforcement.

For Taft, the battle was done. Wilson, he was convinced, had killed the League of Nations that was his League, too. Taft had no sympathy with Wilson's call to the people to make the election of 1920 a "great and solemn referendum" by voting Democrat James M. Cox into office as President on the Democratic pledge to continue the fight for America to join the League of Nations.

The Republican plank was weak, but to Taft even Warren Harding, about whom he had private doubts, offered more hope of reviving the League. Let the League's disappointed supporters call Taft a "turncoat," as many would, he still meant to campaign for Harding. He had other reasons, of course, centered upon his faith in conservative Republicanism. He had predicted it would take one Democratic term before the people were ready to get rid of the Democrats; it had taken two, but one Democratic President.

In November, war-weary America overwhelmingly answered Harding's call of "Back to Normalcy!" The victory was a Republican landslide: 16,000,000 votes and thirty-seven states for Harding and Vice Presidential nominee Calvin Coolidge, and only 9,000,000 votes and eleven states for Cox and his running mate, Franklin D. Roosevelt. Taft's Republican old guard had come back to the White House and would stay there the rest of his life.

With Harding as the new President, Taft had another dream, an older one. For a time he had almost lost it, but now there was a chance after all of the Supreme Court.

** CHAPTER **

20

TAFT and President-elect Harding were both surprised by a breakfast conversation they had in December, 1920, when Taft visited Harding's Marion, Ohio, home. As they ate waffles and creamed chipped beef, Harding offhandedly remarked, "By the way, I want to ask you, would you accept a position on the Supreme Bench, because if you would I'll put you on that Court."

"I was nearly struck dumb," Taft wrote Nellie afterwards. Not that Taft hadn't done all he could through friends to let Harding know he would be available, but he hardly expected such a direct promise only a few weeks after Harding's election. Taft answered that it had always been his ambition. But then he surprised Harding by telling him as frankly, "I could not accept any place but the Chief Justiceship."

At that, Harding was silent. "He said nothing more about it," Taft wrote Nellie, "and I could not make out whether he concluded that was satisfactory or whether he did not further wish to commit himself."

While newspaper rumors of Taft's possible Court appointment boiled behind him, he and Nellie went off for a brief vacation to Bermuda, and he then went on to Montreal, on a leave of absence from Yale, to serve as arbitrator in connection with the taking over of the Grand Trunk Railway by the Canadian government. His friends meanwhile went to work to get Harding to come through with the appointment.

Edward White, whom Taft had made Chief Justice while he was President, had reached the age of seventy-five, was almost deaf, partly blind, and in poor health, and Taft counted on White to retire. They were good friends, White had made it clear that he would like to see Taft succeed him, and they had an informal understanding that if the opportunity came White would step down and make room for him on the Court. But White grew reluctant to hand in his resignation after reporters started asking him how soon he intended to remove himself from the bench, and there was much talk that Harding was considering other men for Chief Justice. The most prominent of the other candidates, Charles Evans Hughes, was eliminated when Harding named him to his cabinet as Secretary of State.

With the chance to be Chief Justice so close after a lifetime of waiting, Taft worried that it might slip from his reach. "I don't hesitate to say to you that I would rather have been Chief Justice than President and that now it would give me the greatest joy to end my career by useful service in that exalted office," he wrote a friend, but added that perhaps he should "suppress my ambitious thoughts" and "settle down to my work at Yale as a graceful ending of my activities. . . . I have children and a wife who gave me joy, and a consciousness of having tried to be useful. What more can I ask?"

On May 19, 1921, Chief Justice White died, and on June 30 President Harding called in the correspondents to announce that he had just sent a clerk to the Capitol to put Taft's nomination as Chief Justice before the Senate. He praised Taft as a man who possessed "a legal mind that would measure up to the eminence of . . . the greatest judicial position in the world." In the Senate, only four of Taft's foes opposed the nomination. Senator William Borah of Idaho tried to lead the "bitter-enders" into battle by charging that

Taft had been a politician and not a practicing lawyer for thirty years. Borah was joined by two other old Republican insurgents, Wisconsin's Robert La Follette and California's Hiram Johnson, and by Democrat Thomas Watson of Georgia. But the Democratic floor leader, Oscar Underwood of Alabama, urged confirmation, and with only four votes against it Taft's nomination was approved by the Senate the same afternoon it came from the White House.

Taft was in Montreal when reporters asked if he was pleased with Harding's choice of a new Chief Justice. He laughed and said, "You can judge for yourselves about that." Later he issued a statement saying he was "profoundly grateful" to the President and pleased by the Senate's immediate confirmation. Now that his lifetime ambition was gratified, he said, "I tremble to think whether I can worthily fill the position and be useful to the country."

He immediately resigned his Yale professorship, but had to remain in Montreal another week to finish the railroad arbitration hearings before he could get to Washington. Despite a minor automobile accident in which his knees were bruised when his car skidded in a Washington rainstorm, Taft displayed what reporters called "the happiest smile of his life" when he appeared at the Capitol on July 11 to take his Constitutional Oath as Chief Justice. His induction would wait until Court began its October session.

Accompanied by his brother, Henry, he went through the brief ceremony in Attorney General Harry Daugherty's office, saved the pen with which he signed the oath to give to Nellie, posed for newsreel photographers, and then went over to the White House to see the President. In the afternoon, he went back to the Capitol to shake hands with old friends in Congress and to inspect the quarters of the Supreme Court in the marble-columned Old Senate Chamber it had occupied since the Civil War.

When reporters asked about his immediate plans, he joked and said the most pressing business before the Chief Justice was to hunt for a house. He sold his New Haven home, and he and Nellie finally found a Washington house they liked at Wyoming Avenue and Twenty-third Street. A spacious, comfortable $75,000 home, with three pleasant and often occupied guest rooms, it later was extensively remodeled so that an elevator could be installed to Taft's third-floor study. In the study, where he had a small library of Federal and English law reports, he hung a portrait of his father, Alphonso.

"We have been wanderers on the face of the earth and it will be good to be anchored in a city we like and where we have so many friends," he wrote. Taft enjoyed walking about the city, and for as long as his health permitted the three-mile morning walk from his home to the Capitol was part of the daily routine that made him a familiar figure to Washingtonians. In late afternoons, he frequently walked through Rock Creek Park, across the ravine where what was later known as the Taft Bridge was built.

But the home he and Nellie still loved best was the one at Murray Bay in Canada, which the Tafts expanded through thirty summers into a place big enough for all the family and friends of his sons and daughter, his five grandchildren, and enough guests to make it seem at times like a summer hotel. It grew into a sprawling rustic house of ten bedrooms, four baths, sitting rooms, downstairs parlors, separate servant quarters, big open fireplaces, and a study for Taft with French windows that opened toward the St. Lawrence and the hills beyond. Through the years, Taft had come to know the French-Canadians of the small settlement by their first names, and they affectionately called him *Le Petit Juge*. For Taft, it was a place to relax in old clothes, to picnic, go on fishing parties, swim, play cards and enjoy good conversation and family fun. During all his Supreme Court years, as each June session neared its end, Taft eagerly longed to be back at Murray Bay. In baggy knickers and a battered hat, he played golf there almost every summer day until his last few years when poor health forced him to be content to sit around the clubhouse and talk the game instead of swinging a club.

On October 3, 1921, when the Supreme Court began its fall term, Taft took the Judicial Oath, which was administered with traditional ceremony by the Court's senior Associate Justice Joseph McKenna. Taft was amused because the clerk who was supposed to furnish Justice McKenna with a copy of the oath became confused and sent up a Bible instead. "The Justice trusted to his memory," he noted, and "it necessitated a little halt . . . but we got through."

Taft began the "incessant labor and great responsibility" that he would describe after six years of it as leaving him "never free from the burden of feeling that whenever I attempt to do anything else I am taking time from my judicial work." His Court duties set the schedule of his daily life. He got up at a quarter past five in the morning and began work at home at six in order to get in two hours of it before breakfast, which was followed by another hour and forty-five minutes at his desk. For exercise he then walked the three miles to the Capitol, and worked in chambers until the Court session began at noon. Court usually lasted until four-thirty, with a half-hour recess for lunch. Afterwards, he was driven home, or walked part way in good weather, and worked at home until dinner, took an hour off, and worked until ten o'clock, when he went to bed. He had to adjust his routine to meet changing activities and after five years of it admitted he was forced to "let up a bit," but nobody again ever accused him of laziness as some critics had when he was President.

Official receptions and social functions were part of his obligation as Chief Justice, but he made it a policy never to allow more than two social evenings in any week, and when he did go out anywhere it usually was to put in a necessary appearance and then to leave for home as soon as possible. Sometimes, but not often when Court was in session, he and Nellie entertained a few old friends at home. He was much more careful about his diet. Having brought his weight down to around 240 pounds during his Yale years, he pretty well managed to keep it there, often by limiting supper to toast and an apple.

His public speeches ended when he became Chief Justice, except for those at occasional official functions or addresses before bar associations. He also had to give up writing articles and had to be careful about interviews. "Things are different now," he explained soon after he became Chief Justice. "Much of what I think must be kept to myself."

He had "taken the veil," he informed friends, when he took his place on the Court. "The Chief Justice goes into a monastery," he said, "and confines himself to judicial work." But Taft was not at all monastic when it came to influencing Presidents, Congressmen, editors, and important friends in all manner of high places to put across his ideas and carry them out for what he believed was the good of the Court. He was the best lobbyist the Supreme Court ever had.

✳ CHAPTER ✳

21

CHIEF JUSTICE TAFT's idol, a man he often quoted, was the great John Marshall, the statesman of the Court, who a century before had made the Court supreme. Taft was no Marshall, as he probably would have been the first to admit, but in their lives there were interesting parallels. Both came to the Court with political experience and used the Court as an instrument to support their philosophies of government. Both also exalted the position and prestige of the Court with broad concepts of the office of Chief Justice that added to its formal and informal powers and sometimes strained traditional authority to its limit.

Few Chief Justices, Taft included, matched Marshall's intellect and style, or his broad vision of the Constitution as ever responsive to the changing needs of the people. But few since Marshall had brought to the Chief Justiceship a more expansive view of its duties and responsibilities than Taft. He worked not only within the Supreme Court but on many fronts outside it to uplift and guard its place in government, and to strengthen the influence of the Chief Justice over all the nation's courts and law. He also worked to make the Court a stronghold of his own conservative views.

Taft was the very image of authority, in physical appearance, in personality, and because of his prominence as a former President. On the bench, or wherever he appeared in public, he commanded respect. In the courtroom, he insisted upon it, to preserve the dignity he considered important to public veneration of the Supreme Court. He was acutely sensitive even to small departures from formality.

Attorneys who appeared before the Court were given to understand that they must dress properly in dark suits, wear vests to cover their neckties or else tuck the ends of their ties into their belts and keep their jackets buttoned, and that they were to leave hats, umbrellas and other personal gear outside. Taft tolerated neither slovenly appearance nor improper presentation of arguments. He was extremely courteous and patient with attorneys who presented legally well-constructed cases. Those who didn't usually were interrupted by a string of probing legal questions. They knew they were in for a stern going-over by the Chief Justice whenever he cleared his throat and started with the words, "What I want to know—"

He almost never lost his temper on the bench, and seldom his sense of humor. When one small-town lawyer, making his first Supreme Court appearance, became flustered and addressed the justices as "Gentlemen" instead of "Your Honors," and then quickly mumbled an apology, Taft put him at ease by saying, "You need not apologize for calling us gentlemen, for that is what we hope we are."

Although he was cautious about his own public conduct and that of his fellow justices, he also believed in "humanizing" the Court. Unlike his predecessors, Taft welcomed the opportunity to join in the fun of such informal affairs as the annual Gridiron dinners given by Washington correspondents. Judges, he held, are "only human," but he also said, "A Chief Justice has to be more circumspect than Caesar's wife, and life is so varied for him that there are many pitfalls." The prestige of his Court, Taft wrote, "next to my wife and my children, is the nearest thing to my heart in life."

While he took no public part in politics, his influence with Presidents Harding, Coolidge and Hoover was direct and personal. Taft was frequently at the White House, not only to promote Court matters, but as a former Republican President whose advice often was sought on policy decisions and patronage. Between visits, he exchanged notes with the Presidents, sometimes suggested what should go into important speeches and messages, and gave his views on the handling of administration measures.

His immediate interest when he became Chief Justice was in speeding up and making more efficient the machinery of the Federal courts in general and the Supreme Court in particular. When it came to judicial decisions, all the Supreme Court Justices had an equal voice, but Taft definitely took charge as chief executive in managing the business of the Court.

He reorganized the staff, urged Congress to increase staff salaries, and had legislation passed to make his own secretary, Wendell Mischler, officially Secretary to the Chief Justice, a title formerly held by a law clerk. Taft changed many old rules to straighten out what he called "absurdities that have been handed down since the beginning of the Court," revised the Court's system of accounting, enforced the collection of fees, and cut the cost of printing Court records by more than one third.

Unlike many Chief Justices before him, he stretched his unwritten powers not only as executive of the Supreme Court but also over the lower courts as Chief Justice of the United States. Pointing out that "I am the head of the judicial branch of government," he announced his determination to organize the courts into a harmonious system by working closely "with the Federal judges of the country so that we may feel more allegiance to a team and do more teamwork." He kept close watch over district and circuit judges, wrote to praise or prod them, and at times even urged judges of high state courts, over whom he had no authority, to speed action on long-delayed cases.

Taft had little patience with lazy judges or with those who were harsh or dictatorial. Every judge, he wrote, "should have constantly before him that the reason for the existence of the courts is to promote the happiness of all the people by speedy and careful administration of justice, and every judge should exert himself to the uttermost to see that in his rulings and in his conduct of business he is . . . making his court . . . useful to the community." He worked to rid the courts "of the burden of complex procedure and delays," saying that "in maintaining equality between the rich and the poor in the court, the greatest difficulty is the delay. A rich man can stand the delay and profits by it, but the poor man always suffers."

As Chief Justice, he had no formal power to decide the choice of lower court judges, and most Chief Justices had avoided being involved in such decisions. But Taft assumed the right to "guide the President" in appointing "sound men" to the Federal courts. At times, he exercised what amounted to veto power over judicial appointments. He received first-hand reports from Federal judges across the country on the qualifications of men who might be appointed, wrote to ask detailed questions about candidates, and held conferences in Washington and elsewhere to discuss possible choices with members of various bar associations. He then made his recommendations to the President and the Attorney General.

He found President Harding's Attorney General Daugherty usually "willing to follow suggestions from me." When Coolidge became President and Daugherty was succeeded by former Columbia Law School Dean Harlan Fiske Stone, Taft lost no time in establishing a relationship with him to win the appointment of judges he recommended. Under President Hoover, Attorney General William Mitchell again invited Taft's advice.

Taft didn't always get the judges he wanted appointed to

the lower courts, but he did block the appointment of many he considered poor choices. He undoubtedly kept dishonest or incompetent men from becoming Federal judges. He also kept some off the bench because they didn't share his conservative views.

When it came to the Supreme Court itself, he was even more anxious to prevent filling vacancies during his time as Chief Justice with new fellow justices who might not share his conservative principles. He all but ignored the tradition, often more a myth than a fact, that a Chief Justice should not indulge in the power politics of choosing those who will occupy the bench with him. As one of the most political of Chief Justices since John Marshall, he used all the influence he could bring to bear, directly and indirectly, to secure the appointment of justices he hoped would agree with him on the basic values of constitutional government and the role of the Court within the political system. He was almost entirely successful in keeping out men he thought might misinterpret the Constitution or increase dissension within the Court.

Of the four justices who came to the bench while he was Chief Justice, the one most campaigned for by Taft was Pierce Butler, a prominent Minnesota attorney and railroad law expert, with whom he became acquainted during the Canadian railroad arbitration case. But Taft also encouraged the appointment of Harding's campaign adviser, former Utah Senator George Sutherland; he approved the promotion from the circuit court to the Supreme Court of Judge Edward T. Sanford, and helped win a place on the Court for Harlan Fiske Stone, who soon was to express views far removed from Taft's, and who in later years would become a Chief Justice himself.

When Taft became Chief Justice, the Supreme Court was badly divided, upset by personal bickering, and almost hopelessly behind in its work. Determined to make the Supreme Court's promptness "a model for the courts of the country," he kept pressure on the justices to speed its business and to bring cases to a quicker hearing. He sometimes lengthened conferences to six hours at a stretch, and even tried, but without success, to get the justices to agree to shorten their summer recess so as to add another week to the Court term. At the end of his first year, he was able to claim that the Court "broke all records in the number of cases disposed of by almost one hundred," and before he finished his years as Chief Justice the Court had reached its most productive work level since before the Civil War.

The real influence of any Chief Justice over the Court rests mainly on his personal character and on the way in which he exercises his leadership in managing the docket, presenting the cases in conference, guiding the discussion, and when in the majority, assigning the writing of opinions. Taft used his powers of assignment effectively, was fair in distributing the burden of work, sensitive to personality conflicts, and respected the knowledge of his fellow justices in special fields of law. He persuaded rather than argued, and showed a reasonable willingness to compromise that often led others to agreement. Soon after he had taken charge, Justice Oliver Wendell Holmes, who had been on the Court almost a quarter of a century, commented, "We are very happy with the present Chief." Four years later, Holmes said that "never before . . . have we gotten along with so little jangling and dissension."

Taft had worried before becoming Chief Justice that he might not get along well with Holmes, whose liberal views were almost the direct opposite of his own. But their personal relations were pleasant from the start, and they eventually became intimate and affectionate friends. Although they continued to disagree, and often sharply, on legal questions and many other things, Taft and Holmes became such friendly foes that they walked or drove to Court together almost every day the rest of Taft's years.

He also had to overcome what had been a long personal feud with Justice Louis Brandeis that dated back to the

Alaskan land fraud controversy when Taft was President and Brandeis was a private attorney for those who brought charges against Secretary of the Interior Ballinger. In 1916 when President Wilson appointed Brandeis to the Court, Taft had joined in an unsuccessful attempt to have the Senate Judiciary Committee block the appointment, calling Brandeis "a Socialist . . . who would break down the Supreme Court."

But the hurts and furies of the Presidential years had cooled, and Taft had overcome his grudge and amended his opinion of Brandeis. He had written Brandeis a cordial note, and Brandeis also was too intelligent to harbor old grudges, so they buried the hatchet. Soon after becoming Chief Justice, Taft wrote, "Brandeis and I are on most excellent terms," and Brandeis, in turn, felt things were "going happily with Taft . . . when we differ, we agree to differ without any ill feeling." By the beginning of his Court's second term, Taft had "come to like Brandeis very much indeed."

Almost in spite of himself, Taft also became fond of Justice John Clarke, another liberal put on the Court by President Wilson. But Taft found his patience sorely tried by Justice James McReynolds, Wilson's former Attorney General, who according to Taft was "selfish to the last degree" and "fuller of prejudice than any man I have ever known." It was an opinion apparently shared by most of the justices, who were infuriated by the way McReynolds made offhand remarks from the Court Bench, bluntly criticized the opinions others wrote, went into rages when he couldn't get his own way, and frequently took off on unannounced vacations that left the Court in a jam. McReynolds was a bitter anti-Semite who made little attempt to conceal his hatred for Brandeis, even to the point of refusing to travel with him to Court ceremonies or to sit next to him for the usual Court photograph. He also hated Clarke, partly because Clarke frequently sided with Brandeis on opinions instead of accepting McReynolds' own ultra-conservative views. When Clarke resigned from the Court in 1922, McReynolds refused to sign the joint letter the justices sent to Clarke, which Taft commented was "a fair sample of . . . the difficulty of getting along with him."

By the fall of 1922, Taft worried that "the Court has been shot to pieces." Justice William Day, who had been appointed by Theodore Roosevelt, had been "doing no work" and was about to resign. So would Justice Mahlon Pitney, who was ill at home. Holmes was in temporarily poor health, Mc-Reynolds had the gout, and Van Devanter had "trouble with his eyes." That meant much reassignment of cases, with the heavy burden of extra work falling on Taft himself.

Van Devanter, whom Taft had appointed to the Court, was the justice he leaned on most. Taft referred to him as "my strength" and "my chancellor," and even confessed wondering whether Van Devanter was not better suited to be Chief Justice than he was himself. But while Van Devanter had keen analytical powers and an intellectual vigor that made him invaluable in conference or in editing his colleagues' opinions, he wrote few opinions of his own. A perfectionist, he was decidedly "opinion-shy," and turned out only a fraction of what the other justices wrote.

Taft was somewhat heartened by the replacements who came to the Court for the three justices who resigned. Sutherland and Sanford, with rare exceptions, stood solidly with him on opinions, and Butler was an unwavering adherent of Taft's "teamwork" policy. Butler assured Taft, "To me it is a genuine pleasure to help, if I can at all, to lessen your load."

A major obstacle to getting work done was the lingering presence on the Court of elderly Justice Joseph McKenna, appointed back in McKinley's time, who was rapidly failing physically and mentally. "In case after case," Taft wrote confidentially, "he had missed the point . . . in one instance he wrote an opinion deciding the case one way when there had been a unanimous vote the other way, including his own." As senior associate justice, McKenna ran the Court in Taft's absence, but the other justices complained that with McKenna in charge nothing was accomplished in conference and the work had to be done all over again when Taft returned.

Taft's own health was not good. In 1922 he was bothered by bladder ailments and early in 1924 he suffered two minor heart attacks, but hurried back to his work at the Court because he felt that McKenna's mental condition made him unable to preside. Taft tried to stay in bed except during the hours Court was in session, but that still did not solve the problem. He had not completely recovered even after a full summer's rest at Murray Bay.

McKenna was extremely sensitive and rejected all polite hints that he should retire. Taft and the other justices were reluctant to hurt his feelings, but the situation had become critical. McKenna was circulating opinions with "language as is fog," Taft noted, "and loses his temper at times and creates . . . scenes in the conference." He pointed out that "McKenna's vote may change the judgment of the Court on important issues" and "he is not able to grasp the point, or give a wise and deliberate consideration of it."

In October, 1924, Taft suffered a third heart attack and decided it was imperative to do something about McKenna. He learned that McKenna's family was anxious to have him retire and consulted McKenna's doctor, who confirmed his incompetence to continue on the Court. Finally Taft called the other justices to a Sunday afternoon meeting at his home, where they decided they would not hand down decisions in cases in which McKenna's vote was pivotal. After recording their "high appreciation of his qualities as a man" and "greatly deploring the necessity for doing this which seemed to be our duty," they authorized Taft to do "as seems best."

He had no authority to request McKenna's resignation, but he gently persuaded him to be "bound by the opinion of his colleagues," and Justice McKenna agreed to retire. Court tradition was ignored to make a special ceremony of accepting his resignation on January 5, 1925, at which a public appreciation for his long services on the Court was read, a basket of roses was placed in front of him, and all the justices stood as McKenna marched out of the courtroom, escorted by the marshal.

On the same day, President Coolidge nominated Harlan Fiske Stone. Taft had been eager to have Stone on the Court but eventually, to Taft's deep disappointment, Stone became one of the frequent liberal dissenters, along with Brandeis and Holmes. Taft shrank from all dissents, including his own. "I would not think of opposing the views of my brethren," he once said, "if there was a majority against my own," and explained at another time, "I think in many cases where I differ from the majority, it is more important to stand by the Court and give its judgment weight than merely to record my individual dissent."

Taft wrote only about twenty dissenting opinions in nine years, and it was even more unusual for him to write a minority opinion. During his Chief Justiceship he suppressed at least an estimated two hundred dissenting votes. Although his Court became constantly torn with dissents, especially in the last years, he usually could round up a safe majority on his side to the very end. He himself wrote about one sixth of the total of 1,596 opinions delivered by the Court while he was Chief Justice, which was far more than any of the other justices.

His taking so much of the Court's opinion writing upon himself, and his unwillingness to spare himself from the smallest detail of administrative work, contributed to the breakdown of his health. Yet with all of his direct Court work as Chief Justice, it was in his labors outside the Court, in the fight for judicial reform, that Taft accomplished the most. On the Court, he generally was a rock-ribbed conservative, but in his zeal to rebuild the nation's court system he was as close as he ever came to being a bold radical.

** CHAPTER **

22

HAVING begun as a farm nation of a few million people, by 1921 America had grown to a booming industrial land of more than one hundred millions, but its Federal court system was still hitched to the plow of the past. Chief Justice Taft, perhaps more than any other individual, reformed it to meet the needs of the twentieth century. On his own initiative, he conceived the program of reform, put it into the language of law, lobbied for it up and down the country, and stalked the halls of Congress until he got much of what he wanted. What he didn't get, he set into motion, paving the way for other changes that would come in time.

It was a battle he had been fighting for more than twenty-five years, as circuit court judge, President, and Yale professor, hammering away at the need for judicial reform in scores of speeches, law review articles, newspaper statements, special messages to Congress, and addresses before bar associations. During nearly all his long public career he had concerned himself profoundly with the need for legislation to improve the Federal courts.

While he was campaigning for the Presidency in 1908, Taft repeatedly called for better administration of the courts, for reducing the load of unimportant cases piled upon the Supreme Court, and for streamlining codes of procedure. As President, in his first message to Congress, he called judicial reform "the greatest need in our American institutions," and outlined recommendations for change. He renewed the call in other messages, tried hard to get his program through, but with his political enemies gaining control of Congress he failed to persuade the politicians or to arouse strong public support.

He had appointed Edward White as Chief Justice while he was President with the hope that White would "go into questions of method . . . and if possible revise the entire procedures of this country," but White turned out to be no judicial reformer. A stickler for proprieties, White avoided using even the mildest pressure as Chief Justice, believing that the strict separation of powers prohibited him from suggesting what changes Congress might make in judicial organization.

As a law professor, both at Yale and in his lecturing around the country, Taft again made the need for judicial reform a favorite theme. His voice and his influence during those years greatly helped build the public support he had lacked as President. There was "a crisis in the life of our courts," he told the people, over and over again. Taft believed the court system of Great Britain offered a blueprint for change. The success of the British system, he pointed out, rested on "executive control vested in a council of judges to direct business . . ."

By 1914, Professor Taft was offering a definite program, the important points of which he would battle into law after he became Chief Justice. "Authority and duty should be conferred upon the head of the Federal judicial system," he proposed, "with the Chief Justice or a council of judges appointed by him . . . to consider each year the pending Federal judicial business of the country." And there "should be a reduction of the appeals to the Supreme Court, by cutting down to cases of constitutional construction . . . and by leaving to the discretion of that Court, by writ of *certiorari,* the power to hear such cases from the lower courts as it deems in the public interest."

Even before the First World War, industrial development, patent suits, the complexes of financial and business growth, and increasing Federal controls over everything from narcotics and auto theft to income tax violations, had clogged court dockets and delayed judgments. Encumbered by a staggering variety of outmoded procedures and lacking any unified direction, the court system had been totally unprepared for the added legal burdens of the war and postwar years.

Wartime violations, espionage cases, witch-hunting anti-Communist raids, postwar suits over canceled contracts, bankruptcies and readjustments, had all but swamped the courts. Prohibition, as Taft had warned, brought such a flood of new enforcement problems and criminal actions that grew out of its associated racketeering activities that the dockets of some courts were crowded with more cases in a month than they could expect to clear in a year.

The entire Federal court system was without central direction or responsibility. Each judge was left to himself, guided mainly by his conscience and his temperament, to decide how to administer the business of his particular court. Even adequate statistics were lacking, so there was little real basis for comparison to inform the public, or to let judges compare the work they were doing with what was being done in other districts.

When Taft became Chief Justice of the United States, he was determined to become in fact, not just in title, chief executive of the judicial branch of government. "The mere increase of courts or judges will not suffice," he wrote. "We must have machinery of a quasi-executive character. . . . We must have teamwork and judges must be under some sort of disciplinary obligation."

Unlike former Chief Justice White, he meant to let few of the traditional proprieties stand in his way. As a man of hard-learned political experience, and as a former President who had done battle for legislation before, Taft knew the paths through Congress. After a quarter of a century of trying, he meant to carry down those paths the most ambitious program for judicial reform since the Federal court system began.

As Chief Justice, Taft properly could not tell Congress what it should do, but he got around that propriety by having Attorney General Daugherty invite him to "render assistance" to a committee of Federal judges and district attorneys that had been appointed to study Federal court problems. Having been "invited" to offer suggestions, Taft presented the first step in his long-planned program, got the committee to approve, and was asked to draw up a tentative bill.

Early in October, 1921, only days after he had taken his place on the bench, Taft appeared before the Senate Judiciary Committee for an informal discussion of what he said was the "need to do something immediately to keep the courts from being swamped." He was careful to explain that he was not appearing as a spokesman for the justices of the Supreme Court, but merely because he had been asked to outline his personal views.

Taft recommended an increase in the number of Federal judges, with the extra judges to be assigned to any district where they were needed, so they could be moved around to meet whatever jams developed in one area or another. There were nearly 150,000 cases pending in the various courts, and he said that the new judges "should be able to make a great hole in overloaded dockets." But far more than that, he explained, was the need to apply the "executive principle."

"A district judge is a power in his community," he said. "He is apt to become a bit indifferent, and to think people are made for courts, not courts for people." Judges had to maintain their independence as far as decisions were concerned, but they needed administrative supervision. As things stood, each judge "paddled his own canoe," he told the Senators, but like other men they needed "the stimulus of inquiry."

What he recommended was an annual conference of the senior judges of the nine Federal circuits, presided over by the Chief Justice, at which there would be an accounting and discussion of the condition in each circuit. District judges and clerks would be required to report the facts and figures concerning their various districts. Many other things were needed, he added, including revision of court procedure, but the yearly meeting would be a start toward "reasonable supervision of the Federal courts."

Bills were introduced and the fight began. Taft appeared as a witness before the House Judiciary Committee as well as the Senate, and less publicly directed an energetic lobby for his program, personally bringing pressures where he thought they were needed. Congress was perfectly willing to go along with the idea of creating more judges, since that would mean more patronage, but there was strong protest against appointing new district judges at large, to be moved as needed to any court in the country, and also against giving the Chief Justice supervision of the courts through an annual conference.

Taft's old enemies, Senators William Borah, Robert La Follette and Hiram Johnson, who had tried to block his confirmation as Chief Justice, leaped to the attack. Borah, along with other foes, including Senators George Norris, Thomas Walsh and John Shields, were firmly entrenched as members of the Senate Judiciary Committee, whose endorsement of his program he had to win. Norris later would become its chairman.

Taft was accused by the Senators of trying to make himself "Commander in Chief" of an "army" of judges who might prowl the country at his will "for political influence and power over the judiciary." Senator Shields declared that the Chief Justice should have no more to do with the lower courts "than does King George." Senator Norris feared that judges brought to Washington for an annual conference at taxpayer expense might be contaminated by the social high-life of wining and dining every evening at "tables of the idle rich." Others criticized Taft's appearances before the House and Senate committees as violating "the spirit if not the letter of the constitutional separation of powers" and warned that the plan was "an entering wedge" to create an all-powerful "judicial machine."

But the courts were in such trouble Congress had to do something. Taft was not given a completely free hand in assigning judges under the law finally enacted on September 14, 1922. The act assigned new judges to twenty-one specific districts and provided that before the Chief Justice could move any of them temporarily to a new locality he would have to obtain a certificate of request from one circuit and a certificate of release from the other.

However he won a far greater victory for the future of the court system in the authorization by Congress of a conference of senior circuit judges, with the Chief Justice as its head. The Act of 1922 marked a new chapter in the administration of the Federal judicial system, its first real coordination under the "executive principle."

Congress recognized that the judiciary had to be directed, but self-directed by an executive committee of the judges, with the Chief Justice in charge. Each judge would remain independent in his own district, but the annual conference would bring together the senior judges from all parts of the country to work out the problems of administering justice. For the first time, there would be adequate statistics, areas of comparison, a profound body of influence for many and varied reforms over the years to come. Chief Justice Taft called the first annual conference for December 27, 1922.

With that much accomplished, he started on the second step of his program for judicial reform, clearing the Supreme Court's docket of a clutter of unimportant cases that robbed its justices of time and energy needed to decide major issues for which the people, the lower courts and Congress looked to the Supreme Court for direction. In many kinds of cases, the Supreme Court could be forced almost automatically to hear appeals, no matter how minor or lacking in general public interest a case might be. What Taft proposed was revolutionary to many Americans. He meant to have the Court decide for itself which cases it would agree to hear.

Again, what he did was all very much in violation of the traditional role of the Chief Justice. But from the end of the Civil War to the time he became Chief Justice, the cases pending before the Supreme Court each year had almost tripled, and when it came to giving the Court control over its own docket he was willing to sidestep traditions. To satisfy the outward proprieties, Chairman Albert Cummins of the Senate Judiciary Committee suggested that Taft appoint a judge's committee to draft a bill. Taft appointed his own Justices Day, Van Devanter and McReynolds to the committee, which then requested the Chief Justice to serve as a member.

The justices framed a tentative law that also was put before the Judiciary Committee of the House, and the House committee expressed its "deep obligation to the Chief Justice and justices of the Supreme Court for their help, not only in preparing this bill, but in explaining it thoroughly." Taft, in addition to testifying before the committees, began explaining the measure to the public, by means of speeches to bar association groups.

He told members of the Chicago bar that it "should be reserved to the discretion of the Supreme Court to say whether the issue . . . is of sufficient importance to justify a hearing of it." Speaking to the New York County Lawyers' Association, he stressed the fact that every case to be considered for a hearing would be thoroughly reviewed, but said, "All the cases which come from the Circuit Courts of Appeals, all the cases which come from the Court of Appeals of the District of Columbia, all the cases which come from the Court of Claims, and a majority of cases from the state supreme courts must get into the Supreme Court on *certiorari,* if they get in at all."

Congressional friends of the measure soon advised that he would be wise to take himself out of the spotlight. His battle for the Act of 1922 had stirred up lasting opposition and his public campaigning for the new measure was increasing it. Taft agreed that it would be smart for him to "shinny on my side" since "some of my old enemies rather resent my being prominent in pressing legislation." He stopped making speeches, but did not stop lobbying.

The measure was so highly technical few members of Congress fully understood it, and it ran into bad timing in view of the coming 1924 election and the concern of politicians with getting votes. Congress debated what was called the "Judges' Bill" for almost three years, while Taft labored for it relentlessly. Senator Thomas Walsh was among those especially alarmed by the idea of giving the Supreme Court power to review the merits of a case before hearing oral argument, and charged that Taft's "appetite for power grows as it is gratified."

But Taft told Nellie that "the way to get legislation through is to continue to fight at each session and ultimately wear Congress out." He put the powerful machinery and organization of the American Bar Association into motion to support the bill. At one point during his vigorous Congressional lobbying he noted that "Van Devanter, McReynolds and I spent two full days at the Capitol, and Van and I one more full day to get the bill through." Even Senator Walsh, its main opponent, finally told his fellow Senators that "I have been accused of standing in the way. . . . I do not feel like standing alone."

Taft appealed to President Coolidge for help and noted that the President "made a direct invitation to Congress" to pass the bill. Before it reached its final vote in the Senate, forty-six state bar associations, the Conference of Appellate Judges, many law school deans, various national, civic and commercial organizations, and eighty-four Congressmen had signed appeals for its passage.

The effect was overwhelming. Taft's foe Borah lined up with Walsh to support the "Judges' Bill" when the vote came on February 13, 1925. Rather than vote against it, La Follette, Norris and Shields failed to appear. A lone dissenting vote by Alabama's Senator J. Thomas Hefflin was cast against it. The bill was written into law by a Senate landslide of 76 to 1.

A new and vital power had been given to the Supreme Court, the right to go through the cases brought before it and to choose the important ones for decision. Other cases, although within the Court's jurisdiction, it would simply refuse to hear. Before lawyers who were pressing a case could even hope for a decision, they would have to file briefs to convince the Court in the first place that it was one worth considering.

The lawyer who hoped to take his case to the Supreme Court would have to file a formal request for the Court to consider it, a petition for a *writ of certiorari,* which was the order the Court might issue to bring the case up from a lower court. If the Supreme Court denied the petition, the case would come to an end in the lower court, and the decision of that court would stand. Only if the Supreme Court granted the writ would the case be brought up from the lower court for full argument and decision. Most petitions would be denied. In later years, out of an annual average of 2,500 petitions put before the Court, 150 or less would be granted for a full hearing.

Much of the time of the justices was to be taken in carefully selecting the cases, but they would have to give no reasons for rejecting those that they decided among themselves raised no important question. By the time Chief Justice Taft retired in 1930, the work of the Supreme Court would be practically current. More important, his Court and future ones would be deciding principles of vital concern, not just to the individuals involved, but to the nation.

Taft was less successful with the third step of his judicial reform program. For years, he had been arguing the need for simple and effective codes of procedure in the Federal courts, to eliminate a mass of unnecessary rules and technicalities that varied from court to court and often enmeshed lawyers and their clients in long and costly litigation. "One great crying need in the United States," he had told Congress while he was President, "is cheapening the cost of litigation by simplifying judicial procedure and expediting final judgment."

Courts were plagued with almost a hundred different systems of procedure, so that a lawyer not expert in Federal practice or in the rules of a particular court might be lost in a maze of writs, pleadings, motions, forms of process, and other legalities. There were so many different statutes and special acts defining the existing rules that Taft called them "almost a trap to catch the unwary." He urged the streamlining of rules so that cases turned more on their merits than on procedural technicalities. The various procedures used in the Federal court system should be unified, he said, and a single form of civil action was needed.

Both as President and professor he had led a drive to empower the Supreme Court to unify Federal rules of procedure in law and equity. This would not be "a delegation of great power to the Supreme Court," he argued, since the Court "in formulating the rules, will of course consult a committee of the bar and a committee of trial judges." He said: "Congress can lay down the fundamental principles that should govern, and then the Court can fill out the details."

As Chief Justice, testifying before the Senate Judiciary Committee on his other judicial reforms in October, 1921, he seized the opportunity to call for "a law making the practice in the Federal courts a code, including both equity and law" so that "you can have one form of action so simple it does not need any knowledge of local practice." Having planted the idea, he soon announced, "I think Congress is ready to undertake the reform. . . . It has been done in England and ought to be done in the Federal courts."

Long an admirer of the British court system, Taft was convinced England had pointed the way. British lawyers had laid down certain principles and then vested power in courts of justice to set details of procedure. What Congress should do, he held, was "to vest the same power in the Supreme Court with reference to the rules of common law and then give that Court the power to blend them into a code."

In the summer of 1922, Chief Justice Taft went to England to make a firsthand study of "the much simpler procedure of the English courts, with a view of securing legislation of this kind in our Federal system." While there he also received three honorary degrees, met the King and Queen as well as innumerable dukes, earls, members of Parliament and other government leaders, had luncheon at 10 Downing Street with Prime Minister Lloyd George and the British cabinet, and was royally entertained at palace balls and ceremonial affairs, including a great formal banquet given in his honor by the American embassy. He and Nellie enjoyed the social activities, but it was mainly a working vacation. Taft conferred about court procedure with nearly all the important barristers and judges of England and returned to the United States more convinced than ever that "the English administration of justice is the best in the world," but he also had decided that "a great deal of what they do (is) entirely impracticable with us."

Many of the changes in procedure he recommended were based on the information he had assembled in England. But it wasn't until May, 1926, that the Senate Judiciary Committee unanimously reported a procedure bill. At first, the chance of passage seemed bright, but although Taft lobbied and fought for it for more than two years, he was unable to win its adoption. For one thing, several of his own justices, including Holmes, Brandeis and McReynolds, were less than enthusiastic about having the Supreme Court spend its time and energy revising the Federal rules of procedures.

Senator Walsh led the opposition that beat back all attempts to enact the procedure bill. Dead set against any uniformity of Federal procedure that might change the rules under which small-town lawyers had always practiced in their own states, Walsh saw the reform as part of an insidious plot to concentrate further power in the Federal courts. It was an attempt to set a precedent by seizing legislative authority from Congress, Walsh warned, so as to put the future control of courts, their organization, rules, jurisdiction, and possibly even salaries, into the hands of judges instead of in control of the elected representatives of the people.

Taft denied such charges in every way he could and declared that the reform was intended only to bring the people better, quicker and less expensive justice. But Congress, ever jealous of its rule-making powers, refused to authorize the revised rules of procedure during Taft's lifetime. He had, however, given the idea momentum, and in 1934 some of the changes he had so long advocated were authorized. Four years after that, in 1938, the Federal Rules of Procedure Act finally became law.

Chief Justice Taft also gave the Supreme Court the first home of its own. Ever since the beginning, the Court had been an orphan as far as housing was concerned, forced to take hand-me-down space in the Capitol building, shifted from place to place according to whatever quarters Congress allowed it to squeeze into. When Taft became Chief Justice, the Court was in the Old Senate Chamber, and committee hearings were crowding it so much that he had to appeal to the Senate "to let the Supreme Court have at least breathing space" because there was not room enough left for its records. "It really is not fair," he complained. "In our conference room the shelves have to be so high that it takes an aeroplane to reach them."

But there was another reason behind his protests, that of making the Senate aware of the fact that what the Supreme Court really needed was a building of its own. He had long dreamed of a Supreme Court building, independent of the other branches of government. "We ought to have a building by ourselves," he wrote, "and one under our control."

He began lobbying for it in earnest when a Senate bill in 1925 authorized spending fifty million dollars for new public buildings. His Senate opponents refused to agree, but while the bill was still in conference to settle differences between the two branches of Congress, Taft went to work to convince members of the House committee. He succeeded, and the final version of the bill, signed by President Coolidge, called upon the Secretary of the Treasury to acquire a site for the Supreme Court.

Taft kept after the Senate Public Lands and Surveys Committee for another year before it passed necessary resolutions so that by 1928 the plot for the building had been purchased. He then lobbied to remove the planning from the Capitol architect's office so it could be put in charge of "an architect of national reputation." After much political maneuvering by Taft, President Coolidge signed a bill making the Chief Justice and Justice Van Devanter members of the building commission. That gave Taft almost full say over the building, the selection of architect Cass Gilbert, and supervision of construction under the Supreme Court's control to meet its own needs. He still had to overcome budget-slashing attacks on the plan, the continuing antagonism of some Senators, general lack of public interest, and the reluctance of some of his own justices to move from their traditional place in the Capitol to a new "marble palace."

By late 1929, Taft's health was failing rapidly and he wondered if he would live to see the new building started, but as ill as he was he was determined to make sure it would be built. He went back to lobbying again to make sure actual construction funds were appropriated. When Congress at last allocated $9,740,000 for it, and President Hoover signed the measure on December 17, 1929, Taft knew that even though he might never see it, there would be a Supreme Court building. "This has been a great week for me," he said. "I was really deeply gratified."

At the cornerstone laying ceremony for the new Supreme Court Building in October, 1932, then Chief Justice Hughes said, "For this enterprise now progressing to completion . . . we are indebted to the late Chief Justice William Howard Taft more than anyone else. This building is the result of his intelligent persistence."

** CHAPTER **

23

CHIEF JUSTICE TAFT in his first major opinion, delivered soon after he had taken his place on the Supreme Court in 1921, made clear his conservative views of the Constitution as a fixed and unchanging barrier to attempts by the states to experiment with liberal social legislation. His dissenting fellow justices, Holmes and Brandeis, made it equally clear that they disagreed with his narrow interpretation.

Under question in the landmark case of *Truax vs. Corrigan* was the constitutionality of an Arizona law that barred the courts of that state from issuing injunctions against labor unions to halt boycotting and picketing. The case grew out of a labor dispute five years before between union waiters and the owner of a Bisbee, Arizona, restaurant called The English Kitchen. Owner William Truax complained that some of his former employees so intimidated him, his non-union help and the patrons that the restaurant lost more than forty thousand dollars in a year. He charged that rumors were spread by the union to destroy the restaurant's reputation, customers were insulted and struck by pickets, and that some of his help were chased down Bisbee's streets at the point of a butcher's knife.

When Arizona's courts refused to enjoin Restaurant Workers' Union leader Michael Corrigan and his fellow unionists from what Truax claimed were "illegal activities," lawyers for Truax challenged the constitutionality of the Arizona anti-injunction law on the grounds that it was class legislation which favored unions and failed to give employers equal legal rights. Any such law passed by a state legislature, they argued, violated the Fourteenth Amendment of the Constitution of the United States by depriving people of their property without due process of law and by denying them equal protection of the laws.

Chief Justice Taft's Supreme Court agreed by a slim majority. In his lengthy opinion, Taft held that "business is a property right," and that "free access for employees, owner, and customers to his place of business is incident to such right." He said, "A law which operates to make lawful such a wrong as is described in plaintiffs' complaint deprives the owner of the business and the premises of his property without due process, and cannot be held valid under the Fourteenth Amendment." In what amounted to a statement of his constitutional creed, Taft said: "When fundamental rights are thus attempted to be taken away . . . we may well subject such experiment to attentive judgment. The Constitution was intended, its very purpose was, to prevent experimentation with the fundamental rights of the individual."

So the Court held that the Arizona law, and other such controls by state legislatures, could not be allowed. But Justices Pitney and Clarke, as well as Holmes and Brandeis, refused to go along with Taft's opinion. Holmes did not agree with Taft's definition of business as "property . . . like land," and argued that business was merely "a course of conduct." He cautioned against "the use of the Fourteenth Amendment beyond the absolute compulsion of its words to prevent the making of social experiments that an important part of the community desires." Dissenting from Taft's view that the Constitution was intended to bar legislative experiments, Holmes said: "Legislation may begin where an evil begins."

Brandeis also admonished the Court not "to close the

door to experiment within the law." The law of property, he held, "was not appropriate for dealing with the forces beneath social unrest" and he said that the "rights of property and the liberty of the individual must be remolded, from time to time, to meet the changing needs of society."

Many of Taft's opinions were to reflect a narrow and restrictive interpretation of the Constitution. Yet his views were progressive and liberal in interstate commerce opinions, some of which pointed the way for the Supreme Court of another decade to uphold much of the legislation of Franklin Roosevelt's New Deal.

As an advocate of broad Federal powers under the commerce clause of the Constitution, Chief Justice Taft placed himself squarely in the tradition of his idol, John Marshall. Taft, like Marshall, held that Congress was almost unrestricted in the regulation of interstate commerce. Once it was proven, in any given case, that Federal Powers of regulation rested upon commerce that *was* interstate, Taft believed that the "power of Congress in this respect is . . . exactly what it would be in a government without states."

John Marshall, back in 1824, had ruled that the power of Congress to regulate interstate commerce was absolute, and for years the Supreme Court generally had gone along with Marshall's concept in its decisions limiting state action. Then in 1887 Congress had enacted the Interstate Commerce Act, its first major effort to use the commerce power to control and regulate, followed three years later by the far broader Sherman Antitrust Act.

But Chief Justice Fuller, in the Sugar Trust Case of 1895, had curtailed Marshall's broad concept of commerce, narrowing Federal power mainly to transportation, and holding that manufacturing was a local activity and therefore beyond the reach of Congress. Other Court decisions had continued to restrict Federal powers of regulation under the commerce clause.

Associate Justice Holmes had pointed toward a return to

the view of commerce as a "current" flowing through the states in the case of *Swift vs. United States* in 1905, holding that a combination of meat packers was unlawful. Commerce, Holmes wrote, was "not a technical, legal conception, but a practical one, drawn from the course of business."

Taft, in the Marshall tradition, writing his second major opinion in 1922, restored manufacture and traffic in goods to the broad concept of commerce. He also declared, in effect, that it was for Congress and not the Supreme Court to decide how it should use its power to regulate interstate commerce.

Popularly known as the Stockyards Case, *Stafford vs. Wallace* came before the Supreme Court as a test of the Federal government's right to regulate practices in the Chicago meat packing industry under the Packers and Stockyards Act of 1921. The act sought to regulate business done by the packers in interstate commerce, so there would be a free flow of livestock from cattle ranges and farms through the stockyards and finally to the nation's consumers of meat and meat products. According to Congress, the chief evil that required regulation was a monopoly of packers "enabling them unduly and arbitrarily to lower prices to the shipper who sells, and unduly and arbitrarily to increase the price to the consumer who buys."

Taft upheld the Packers and Stockyards Act on the grounds that while the meat packers might claim they were operating a local business in Chicago in a geographic sense, their activities in an economic sense were only an incident in a continuing interstate market. He held that applying the commerce clause of the Constitution was a perfectly proper result "of the natural development of interstate commerce under modern conditions" and that "it was the inevitable recognition of the great central fact that such streams of commerce from one part of the country to another, which are ever flowing, are, in their very essence, the commerce among the states . . . which historically it was one of the chief purposes of the Constitution to bring under national protection and control."

In words that echoed Marshall's, Taft said: "The stock-yards are not a place of rest or final destination. Thousands of head of livestock arrive daily by carload and trainload lots, and must be promptly sold and disposed of and moved out to give place to the constantly flowing traffic that presses behind. The stockyards are but a throat through which the current flows, and the transactions which occur therein are only incidents to this current from the West to the East, and from one state to another. Such transactions cannot be separated from the movement to which they contribute. . . . The sales are not in this aspect merely local transactions. They create a local change of title, it is true, but they do not stop the flow. . . . The stockyards and sales are necessary factors in the middle of the current of commerce."

Again, almost with Marshall's boldness in declaring Federal supremacy, Taft claimed for Congress a wide area of power that should be free of interference by the courts. He said: "Whatever amounts to more or less constant practice, and threatens to obstruct or unduly burden the freedom of interstate commerce is within the regulatory power of Congress under the Commerce Clause, and it is primarily for Congress to consider and decide the fact of danger and meet it. This Court will certainly not substitute its judgment for that of Congress in such a matter unless the relation of the subject to interstate commerce and its effect upon it are clearly non-existent."

He stated his bold conception of the commerce power once more in 1923 in an opinion upholding government regulation of grain trading on the Chicago Board of Trade. Taft held in *Board of Trade of Chicago vs. Olsen* that Congress had a perfect right, as a matter of regulating interstate commerce, to forbid trading in grain futures except under the supervision of the Secretary of Agriculture.

In decision after decision, his opinions augmented the commerce powers of Congress. Upholding the National Motor Theft Act, which made it a crime to transport a stolen automobile in interstate commerce, he said in 1925: "Congress can certainly regulate interstate commerce to the extent of forbidding or punishing the use of commerce as an agency to promote immorality, dishonesty or the spread of any evil or harm to the people of other states from the state of origin."

His constitutional jurisprudence furnished substantial foundations for events that were to come after he died. When the Supreme Court upheld the Wagner Act of 1935, creating the National Labor Relations Board, it leaned heavily on commerce precedents set by Taft. Yet he also set precedents in opinions dealing with other powers of the Constitution that pointed the way for a later Court to knock down some vital emergency legislation, including the first Agricultural Administration Act in the early New Deal years.

The restrictions Taft put upon Congress in opinions dealing with the use of its taxing power to regulate social and economic evils were as narrow as his commerce opinions had been broad. His views on taxation reflected none of John Marshall's nationalism. Congress, he feared, might use tax penalties as a weapon to regulate almost anything and everything, and thus bring under Federal control many of the rights reserved to the states and to the people by the Constitution. Taft's first major opinion on such taxing powers unfortunately involved an attempt by Congress to halt the use of child labor.

Just before Taft became Chief Justice, the Supreme Court had ruled unconstitutional an act of Congress that barred products of child labor from interstate commerce. Congress then tried again, by passing a second Child Labor Act in 1919, based on tax controls rather than on the commerce clause. It imposed a ten per cent excise tax "in addition to all other taxes" on the net profits of any mine, quarry, mill, cannery, workshop, factory or other business that hired children under the age of fourteen as workers, regardless of the number of children involved.

The act also set up an elaborate code regulating employment of children between the ages of fourteen and sixteen, to prohibit late night hours or extensive overtime work, specifying what would be allowed in certain industries. Never before had Congress tried to establish such national rules of business conduct with the penalty of heavy extra taxes for those who violated them.

Under the new law, the Drexel Furniture Company of North Carolina had some $6,300 assessed against it on the government's claim that during 1919 a boy under the age of fourteen had worked in the furniture factory. In a test of the law's constitutionality, the case of *Bailey vs. Drexel Furniture* was brought before the Supreme Court. On May 15, 1922, Chief Justice Taft and a nearly unanimous Court struck down the Child Labor Law by ruling that it did violate the Constitution.

Taft succeeded in getting even his frequent dissenters, the liberal Brandeis and Holmes, to vote with him. Associate Justice Clarke alone disagreed, and he remained silent as to his reasons and wrote no dissenting opinion. As a humane individual Taft sympathized with the good intentions of the law, but as Chief Justice he believed it raised a grave challenge to the Tenth Amendment of the Constitution, which pledged: "The powers not delegated to the United States by the Constitution, nor prohibited by it to the states, are reserved to the states respectively, or to the people."

As Taft saw it, the basic question was whether Congress had merely imposed an excise tax with only "incidental restraint and regulation," or whether it was trying to regulate "by the use of the so-called tax as a penalty." It was more than just a tax, he said, because it provided "a heavy exaction for a departure from a detailed and specified course of conduct in business" that would force an employer "to pay to the government one-tenth of his entire net income . . . whether he employs five hundred children for a year, or employs only one for a day."

The Court would have to be blind, Taft said, "not to see

that the so-called tax is imposed to stop the employment of children within the age limits prescribed." Its effect and purpose were clearly "prohibitory and regulatory." When all others "can see and understand this," he asked, "how can we properly shut our minds to it?"

It was "the high duty and function of this Court," he said, "to decline to recognize or enforce seeming laws of Congress dealing with subjects not entrusted to Congress but left . . . by the supreme law of the land to the control of the states. We can not avoid the duty even though it requires us to refuse to give effect to legislation designed to promote the highest good. The good sought in unconstitutional legislation is an insidious feature because it leads citizens and legislators of good purpose to promote it without thought of the serious breach it will make in the ark of our covenant or the harm which will come from breaking down . . . the maintenance of local self government, on the one hand, and the national power on the other . . ."

"Grant the validity of this law," he warned, "and all that Congress would need to do, hereafter, in seeking to take over to its control any one of the great number of subjects of public interest . . . would be to enact a detailed measure of complete regulation of the subject and enforce it by a so-called tax . . . To give such magic to the word 'tax' would be to break down all constitutional limitations of the powers of Congress and completely wipe out the sovereignty of the state."

Public feeling strongly favored the Child Labor Law that the Court had killed and Taft was denounced in some newspapers as a protector of greedy employers who exploited children for profit. Some respected jurists also scorned his legal reasoning, claiming it was not the business of the Court to try to guess what motive Congress had in passing a tax law, and saying that for the first time in history Taft had made legislative motive a test of legislative action. During the New Deal years to come, armed with Taft's precedent, the Court would be able to raise the question of "valid motive" in ruling on attempts by Congress to control things previously controlled by the States.

But Taft was convinced he had written good law. Thirty years later it was still influencing other Court opinions. In 1953, Justice Felix Frankfurter, quoting Taft's words, called his reasoning "significant," in vigorously dissenting from the Court's approval at that time of a law forcing gamblers to get a Federal license and pay a tax. Frankfurter said time seemed to be bearing out Taft's warning that Congress might use its taxing power so the Federal government could take over subjects traditionally within the police power of the states.

CHIEF JUSTICE TAFT'S most important dissent from a majority of his own Court was in a strongly liberal position he took in 1923 in favor of an attempt by Congress to set minimum wage standards for women laborers in the District of Columbia to protect them from conditions that "endangered health and morals."

Congress had passed a law in 1918 setting up a Minimum Wage Board to fix and enforce basic cost-of-living pay scales for Washington's working women. One of the Board's first decisions boosted the wages of scrubwomen at the city's Children's Hospital. When the hospital challenged the constitutionality of the law and got the District Court of Appeals to enjoin the board from enforcing the pay hike, the board appealed to the Supreme Court in the case of *Adkins vs. Children's Hospital.*

The Supreme Court majority ruled against the Minimum Wage Law in an opinion by Justice Sutherland, holding that Congress had violated the due process clause of the Fifth Amendment by "unconstitutional interference" with the individual liberty of a worker and his employer "to freely contract with one another in respect of the price for which one shall render service to the other."

Wages, Sutherland held, were a "purely private" matter of equal bargaining between worker and employer and women needed no special protection in deciding what pay to accept. The Court did not find that there was any "public interest" emergency involved which required Congress to become the guardian of women's health or morals by guaranteeing them a basic living wage. Sutherland brushed aside earlier Court opinions that had upheld various laws setting maximum working hours and asserted that fixing pay scales was a different matter. The Minimum Wage Law, he said, was "simply and exclusively a price-fixing law, confined to adult women . . . who are legally as capable of contracting for themselves as men." He held that the right "to contract about one's affairs is part of the liberty of the individual" protected by the due process clause of the Fifth Amendment, and that in making "contracts of employment of labor . . . the parties have an equal right to obtain from each other the best terms they can as a result of private bargaining."

Sutherland's opinion was to influence the Court for a long time in dealing with other attempts to set minimum wage laws. Justice Brandeis did not sit on the case because his daughter was secretary of the Minimum Wage Board that was involved, but Holmes joined Taft in dissenting from the Court majority.

Taft, in his forthright dissent, attacked Sutherland's opinion for using legal technicalities that were "formal rather than real." He said the evils of long hours and low pay under sweatshop conditions of labor were well known and that it was a fallacy to consider women workers the equals of their employers when it came to bargaining for pay. Women who were "in the class receiving least pay" were not on a level of "equality of choice with their employer" because the necessities of their circumstances made them "prone to accept pretty much anything that is offered," he said. "They are peculiarly subject to the overreaching of the harsh and greedy employer."

He admitted there might be some doubt as to whether a

minimum wage law really would correct such employment evils. "But it is not the function of this Court to hold Congressional acts invalid simply because they are passed to carry out economic views which the Court believes to be unwise or unsound," he said. He could not go along with the Court decision that there was a supposed difference between laws that regulated working hours and those that set minimum wages. Taft said there was "respectful authority" to show that long hours of labor and low wages "are equally harmful." But again, he said that was not something for the Court to decide. "Congress took this view and we cannot say it was not warranted in so doing."

But in another opinion he wrote the same year, in the case of *Wolff Packing Company vs. Court of Industrial Relations of Kansas,* Taft took a more conservative view of the right to regulate labor relations. Involved was a state law rather than an act of Congress.

Because of the economic unrest that followed the First World War, the Kansas legislature in 1920 decided to force the arbitration of labor disputes in five types of businesses it classified as "affected with a public interest." It created an industrial court of three judges to deal with any labor controversies that might interfere with the production of food, clothing or fuel, the transportation of those products, and the operation of public utilities and common carriers. The judges, on their own initiative, could summon employers and workers, decide on any dispute between them, and fix wages that the company had to accept and against which the workers were not allowed to strike.

The Charles Wolff Meat Packing Company, faced with a temporary drop in business, cut wages. Union workers protested to the Kansas Industrial Court and the judges restored the wage cuts, even though they conceded that the company would have to operate its business at a loss until more prosperous times. Wages had to be kept high, the state judges ruled, to end the labor dispute that might interfere with the supply of meat to the public.

The company protested that such an edict violated the Constitution's Fourteenth Amendment, which declared: "No state shall make or enforce any law which shall . . . deprive any person of . . . liberty or property without due process of law." When the Kansas Supreme Court ordered the company to obey the state ruling, the case was brought to the United States Supreme Court.

Chief Justice Taft, this time with the whole Court unanimously behind him, decided that the Kansas Industrial Court Act was unconstitutional. The "mere declaration by a "legislature" could not turn a private business into a public one, he said, and the amount of regulation that could be permitted "depends on the nature of the business, on the feature which touches the public, and on the abuses reasonably to be feared."

A public inn or cab system, he pointed out, might be regulated in a far different way than a gas company or a railroad. "To say that business is clothed with a public interest is not to import that the public may take over its entire management and run it at the expense of the owner," he said. It would be "running the public interest argument into the ground" to allow a legislature, just by saying so, to clothe "the common callings" of general business "with full and comprehensive regulation" under which the "employer is bound . . . to pay the wages fixed and . . . the worker . . . is forbidden on penalty of fine or imprisonment to strike against them."

Business, he said in effect, could be regulated by the states only when there was clear proof in each specific case that it was "affected with a public interest." Taft declared: "It has never been supposed, since the adoption of the Constitution, that the business of the butcher, or the baker, the tailor, the woodchopper . . . was clothed with such a public interest that the price of his product or his wages could be fixed by state regulation."

Three years later, with Taft casting the vote that gave it a majority of five, the Court threw out a New York law which forbade theater ticket brokers to collect more than fifty cents above box-office rates, again on the grounds that it violated the Fourteenth Amendment, since a theater as a place of entertainment served no urgent public need. But Justices Holmes, Brandeis, Stone and Sanford, who had supported Taft's views three years before, all dissented.

The tide was beginning to turn toward a more liberal view of state regulations. After a series of decisions, sometimes one way and sometimes the other, the Court eventually would all but read out of constitutional law the narrow distinction "affected with a public interest," and would generally take the position that a state was free to adopt whatever regulations would reasonably promote the public welfare.

** CHAPTER **

25

Among all his opinions, the one Chief Justice Taft considered his most important was delivered in October, 1926, when a divided Supreme Court handed down a decision significant in America's constitutional history by upholding the power of the President to remove from office executive officers of the United States without consent of the Senate.

Ironically it also was an opinion by which former Republican President Taft vindicated former Democratic President Andrew Johnson on the main issue involved in Johnson's impeachment by Republicans more than half a century before. And after Taft's time, Democratic President Franklin Roosevelt was to make use of Taft's opinion in an attempt of his own to remove an official from office.

The President's power of removal had been a vexed question since the writing of the Constitution. Back in the beginning days of Reconstruction that followed the Civil War, the Radical Republicans who dominated the entire Federal government and who tried to strip Andrew Johnson of all Presidential powers, based their unsuccessful impeachment trial mainly on Johnson's defiance of the Tenure of Office Act of 1867.

The act was passed by the Republican Congress to force

President Johnson to keep Secretary of War Edwin Stanton in his cabinet, and when Johnson finally attempted to oust Stanton the furious Republicans tried and failed to throw the President out of the White House. President Johnson hoped at the time to bring the case before the Supreme Court because he was convinced that the Court would rule the Tenure of Office Act unconstitutional, but Republicans blocked his efforts to get a Court hearing. Not until 1926 did the Court, and Chief Justice Taft, make the ruling that vindicated Andrew Johnson.

But Taft's main purpose was not to clear the reputation of Andrew Johnson, but to reinforce for all Presidents what he judged to be the clear constitutional power that gave a President the right to remove an appointed official without consent of the Senate. The 1926 case of *Myers vs. United States* grew out of the dismissal by President Woodrow Wilson in 1920 of Frank S. Myers, whom Wilson had appointed three years before that as postmaster of Portland, Oregon.

Myers, who died before the Supreme Court reached its decision, was appointed Portland's postmaster under an 1876 act of Congress which provided that a postmaster was to hold his position for a four-year term unless dismissed before then by the President "by and with the advice of the Senate." Myers had not served his four years when President Wilson ordered his removal. The Senate did not consent, so Myers sued to recover full pay for the unfinished term. When the Court of Claims turned him down, he appealed to the Supreme Court.

The government answered that a President did not need Senate consent to fire an executive officer such as a postmaster and argued that the 1876 law was unconstitutional. Congress, it was claimed, had no right to pass any law that abridged the executive removal power of the President as implied by the Constitution. But the Constitution did not spell out exactly what that power was. Chief Justice Taft hoped to do so.

"I have really worked on it for a full year or longer," he

noted when he had completed the first draft of his opinion in 1925, after spending most of the summer at Murray Bay researching the history of American government to support his views. As President himself, Taft had become convinced that there was a need for absolute removal power to assure "unity and coordination in executive administration essential to effective action." He hoped as Chief Justice to bring the Court unanimously behind his decision that the 1876 act of Congress was unconstitutional. But Justices Holmes, Brandeis and McReynolds disagreed.

Differences over the case were bitter for a time, and Taft's feelings about it were so strong that the split in the Court, which was already dividing over many issues, grew wider. He was particularly critical of Brandeis, who argued that the Constitution's purpose in separating the branches of government was not to promote administrative efficiency, but to provide "inevitable friction" among the three branches "to save the people from autocracy." Holmes, in his dissent, thought Taft's arguments, drawn from the executive power granted by the Constitution, were "spider's webs inadequate to control the dominant facts."

Afterwards there were many critics who did not agree with Taft's historical analysis, or with all of his legal conclusions. But in writing his opinion, Taft made no concessions. He held that the President's removal power was almost absolute. With a 6 to 3 decision, the Court ruled that the provision of the law of 1876 "by which the unrestricted power of removal of first-class postmasters is denied to the President is in violation of the Constitution and is invalid."

Taft's opinion explored the history of the President's removal power at great length. He went back to debates in the first Congress in 1789 to show that the Founding Fathers intended the President to have "administrative control of those executing the laws" and that "to hold otherwise would make it impossible for the President in case of political difference . . . with the Senate or Congress to take care that the laws be faithfully executed."

He said that just such a thing had happened during the period in history when Andrew Johnson had his political troubles and when "both houses of Congress attempted to reverse this constitutional construction and to subject the power of removing executive officers . . . to the control of the Senate." Taft said that the intentions of the Founding Fathers, who "framed the Constitution and presented it for ratification" and of "the Congress that launched the government" could not be set aside for those of the Congress in Johnson's time which had been motivated by the heat of its political quarrel with the President. The Court would not accept the acts of Johnson's political enemies as valid.

Therefore, Taft declared in effect, since President Johnson had been within his legal rights when he removed Secretary of War Stanton, so was President Wilson within his rights in dismissing postmaster Myers. Said the Chief Justice: "We have no hesitation in holding . . . that the Tenure of Office Act of 1867, in so far as it attempted to prevent the President from removing executive officers who had been appointed by him . . . was invalid, and that subsequent legislation to the same effect was equally so."

The "illimitable power of removal" that Taft's decision had given Presidents was slightly limited after President Franklin Roosevelt tried to use it in October, 1933, to remove William E. Humphrey from the Federal Trade Commission, to which he had been appointed for a seven-year term by President Hoover. Roosevelt asked Humphrey to resign "because I do not feel that your mind and my mind go along together," and when the commissioner refused to quit Roosevelt wrote him: "Effective as of this date you are hereby removed."

Humphrey insisted that Roosevelt could not remove him, remained on the job, and demanded his $10,000 yearly pay. The case went before the Supreme Court of which Hughes had become Chief Justice, and the government attorneys for

President Roosevelt put their chief reliance on Taft's opinion in *Myers vs. United States*. But the Court, in a 1935 ruling, found that the "actual decision in the *Myers* case . . . goes far enough to include all purely executive officers. It goes no farther."

Not included was "an officer who occupies no place in the executive department and who exercises no part of the executive power vested by the Constitution in the President." A Federal Trade Commissioner performed no duties for the President, but was part of an independent, non-partisan administrative and judicial body created by Congress to carry out its legislative programs, the Court said, and therefore Humphrey could not be removed by President Roosevelt.

"Whether the power of the President to remove an officer shall prevail over the authority of Congress . . . will depend upon the character of the office," the 1935 Court decided. But it agreed that those who serve the President in any of the units of the executive department were still subject, as Taft had said, to "the power of the President alone to make the removal."

✴✴ CHAPTER ✴✴

26

CHIEF JUSTICE TAFT'S last major opinion, in a Prohibition era bootlegging case, was also perhaps his most severely criticized, both by the public and by four of his fellow justices. It dealt with what in 1928 was the new question of wiretapping to obtain evidence, a question that was to be raised often through the years in courts, legislatures and Congress, and one that would continually find conflicting answers. Taft's opinion provoked a dissent by Justice Brandeis that became more famous than the opinion itself, and that first brought into constitutional jurisprudence the suggestion of an important new constitutional right, the legal right to privacy.

Before the nation began its tragically unsuccessful attempt to prohibit alcoholic beverages, Taft publicly and consistently opposed Federal regulation of the liquor traffic on the grounds that trying to impose temperance by national law would be almost impossible to enforce, and that it would create widespread graft, corruption and general disrespect for law.

But by the time he became Chief Justice the Eighteenth Amendment was the law and the Supreme Court already had upheld the Volstead Act as constitutional. As a man of law and a life-long opponent of criminal evasion of justice, Taft was especially aroused by the national lawlessness that resulted from Prohibition, and he gradually became a passionate zealot for its enforcement. He tried to make his Court the stern upholder of the government men who fought a losing battle against the flood of illegal alcohol and the rise of organized crime. The other justices also believed in law enforcement, but their dissents from Taft grew stronger as they protested against invasions of liberty for the sake of Prohibition.

Prohibition divided not only Taft's Court, but also his friends, and even his own home. His wife became an outspoken foe of the Eighteenth Amendment that he was trying to enforce. "The truth is that Nellie and I differ on Prohibition," he wrote his brother Horace. "We might as well face that, because I am utterly out of sympathy with her and she with me."

But the fact that others were losing faith in a law that was part of the Constitution, one that he himself had predicted would never work, made it no less the law to him. Taft became even more determined to fight every violation of Prohibition. In a string of decisions, he influenced a Court majority to rule that there was no double jeopardy involved in punishing Prohibition violators in both state and Federal courts, that automobiles could be searched without a warrant when there was reasonable grounds to believe they carried liquor, that mere possession of liquor for personal use could be held a crime by a state, and that the government had a right to limit the amount of liquor a physician could prescribe for medicinal use. His crusade for strict enforcement of criminal law reached its zenith in the wiretapping case of *Olmstead vs. United States.*

Gangland crime, feeding on the profits of bootlegging, was spreading its violence and its rackets; there was widespread corruption of the police, the courts and officials, high and low. Exactly the lawlessness that Taft deplored seemed to be involved in the case. Roy Olmstead had been accused by the government of conspiracy to violate the Prohibition act, and was said to be the head of a bootleg ring that operated around Seattle, selling an annual two million dollars' worth of liquor smuggled in from British Columbia.

Four Federal agents had tapped telephone lines leading to a Seattle office building, and over a period of months had intercepted calls for liquor orders, which led to the conviction of Olmstead and others. None of the wiretapping had been done on the premises of the building itself, but lawyers for the accused men claimed that the tapping of private telephone lines to obtain evidence was an invasion of the defendants' rights under the Constitution's search-and-seizure clause of the Fourth Amendment and of the self-incrimination clause of the Fifth Amendment.

The Supreme Court, by a close 5 to 4 majority refused to treat wiretapping as an unreasonable search and seizure, and ruled that wiretap evidence could be admitted even if it was obtained illegally. Dissenting were Justices Brandeis, Holmes, Stone, and even Taft's usually strong supporter, Butler. Taft, in his opinion for the majority, held that the Fourth Amendment had to be interpreted according to its exact language, which protected a person from unreasonable search of "material things—the person, the house, his papers or effects." But in this case, he said, there had been no trespass, no entry. "The amendment does not forbid what was done here," he said. "There was no seizure. The evidence was secured by the sense of hearing and that only. There was no entry of the houses or offices of the defendants."

He suggested that Congress, if it wished, might pass a law to protect the secrecy of telephone communications by making them inadmissible evidence in Federal court trials. But since there was as yet no such law, he held: "The courts may not adopt such a policy by attributing an enlarged and unusual meaning to the Fourth Amendment. . . . The reasonable view is that one who installs in his house a telephone instrument with connecting wires intends to project his voice to those quite outside, and that the wires beyond his house and while passing over them are not within the protection of the Fourth Amendment."

Taft went back to common law to show that the admissibility of evidence was not affected by whether it had been obtained illegally, pointing out that under the old rule of English courts evidence could be heard no matter how it was obtained. Having already ruled the Fourth Amendment had not been violated, he said the Fifth Amendment's protection against self-incrimination could not be invoked because to allow that would be to subscribe "to the suggestion that the courts have a discretion to exclude evidence, the admission of which is not unconstitutional, because (it was) unethically or illegally secured."

Justice Holmes, in his dissent, held that wiretapping was "such dirty business" no agent of the government should have a hand in it. He pointed out that there was a choice of conflicting principles involved: the need to detect criminals and use all available evidence; and the need to see that "the government should not itself foster and pay for other crimes when they are the means by which the evidence is to be obtained." Said Holmes: "We have to choose, and for my part I think it less an evil that some criminal should escape than that the government should play an ignoble part."

Justice Brandeis, in his famous dissent, in which Justice Stone concurred, severely criticized Taft. "Clauses guaranteeing to the individual protection against specific abuses of power must have a . . . capacity of adaptation to a changing world," he wrote. Time and again the Court had refused to place "unduly literal construction" upon the Fourth Amendment, and he insisted that it should not now close its eyes to invasions of privacy caused by advances in civilization. "Whenever a telephone line is tapped," he said, "the privacy of the persons at both ends of the line is invaded and all conversations between them on any subject . . . although proper, confidential and privileged, may be overheard." Older means of espionage, Brandeis held, were "but puny instruments of tyranny and oppression" when compared with wire-tapping.

The framers of the Constitution would have been appalled by such narrow reading of the Fourth Amendment, Brandeis went on: "They conferred, as against the Government, the right to be let alone—the most comprehensive of rights and the right most valued by civilized men. To protect that right, every unjustifiable intrusion by the Government upon the privacy of the individual, whatever the means employed, must be deemed a violation of the Fourth Amendment. And the use, as evidence in a criminal proceeding, of facts ascertained by such intrusion must be deemed a violation of the Fifth."

It was, Brandeis said, "immaterial that the intrusion was in aid of law enforcement." He said: "Experience should teach us to be most on our guard to protect liberty when the Government's purposes are beneficent. Men born to freedom are naturally alert to repel invasion of their liberty by evil-minded rulers. The greatest dangers to liberty lurk in insidious encroachments by men of zeal, well meaning but without understanding."

Brandeis and Holmes had dissented from Taft's first major opinion as Chief Justice, as they did now from what was to be almost his last opinion of real importance. The Court that Taft had struggled so hard to hold together as a team, with remarkable success for a time, was one he would leave in disharmony, as he had found it.

✱✱ CHAPTER ✱✱

27

WHEN the Supreme Court convened for its October, 1929, term, Chief Justice Taft was back at his old place on the bench, but he had been seriously ill most of the summer at Murray Bay, and his associates were concerned. Late in November, he gave an opinion in a railroad insurance case, and he showed no lack of mental ability to lead the Court or its conferences. He also was able to preside at the annual conference of circuit judges he had established, and he gave much time to considering plans for the new Supreme Court building.

On New Year's Eve he received the saddening news that his brother, Charles, had died in Cincinnati. Against his doctor's advice, Taft insisted that he had to attend the funeral, that he must pay his last respects to the memory of the brother who had helped him through his whole career. Relatives at the funeral said they had never seen Taft more alert. But it was the last time they were to see him so.

The trip to Cincinnati and the emotional strain of the funeral brought him back to Washington so ill that his doctor had to be called when he reached home. Yet there was so much Court work to be done that he tried to go on with it. But by the end of the first week of January, 1930, Justice Van Devanter had to read two opinions Taft had drafted but was unable to deliver.

Finally, Taft agreed to give up work for "two or three weeks" and go to Asheville, North Carolina, to rest and recuperate. He also agreed to go into Washington's Garfield Hospital for a week's treatment before leaving for Asheville. In his absence, Holmes as the senior Justice would preside over the Court. During the week at the hospital, Taft was shielded from all visitors except Nellie, and all Court papers and other correspondence were kept from him. So was the diagnosis of physicians that the state of his health was precarious, with hardening of the arteries far advanced. He was not informed, nor was the general public, but President Hoover was told that if Taft did recover enough to return to the Court, it would not be for long. The President began making plans to choose his successor as Chief Justice.

Under medication, Taft got some sleep and rest, and spent most of his time in the hospital reading detective stories. By the end of the week, he was able to leave the hospital for Asheville. He walked through the long concourse of the Washington station to the train with an easy stride and appeared to reporters to be in a cheerful mood. Nellie, a doctor, nurse, and his secretary made the trip with him, and he was welcomed in Asheville by city officials and by a small crowd of townspeople, to whom he took off his hat and bowed.

He stayed at the Grove Park Inn, where he and Nellie sometimes had gone for brief vacations, and for the first ten days he was able to enjoy daily automobile rides and occasional brief walks in the countryside. But toward the end of January there was a marked change in his condition. Confined to his room, he was barely able to speak at times and could make known only his simplest needs. In more lucid moments, he said he knew he was dying, that he should resign, and that he wanted to return to Washington.

His son Robert was called to Asheville. After a consultation with physicians, he talked to his father. On February 3, 1930, Robert Taft returned to Washington and presented President Hoover with Taft's resignation as Chief Justice. The same day, Taft was carried to a train in Asheville that took him back to Washington.

Taft was pleased when he was told that President Hoover had nominated Charles Evans Hughes as the new Chief Justice. He had appointed Hughes to the Court, gotten him to resign to run for President, and according to his doctor the news that "his own man" now had been put back on the Court to take his place considerably eased Taft's mind, so that he was able to sleep during most of the trip to Washington.

He had been the first Chief Justice to retire voluntarily in 130 years, since Oliver Ellsworth retired in 1800, and the *New York Times* said, "Mr. Taft shows his habitual punctilious sense of honor and public duty in laying down his great office. . . . At this time it may be permitted to remind him that he holds a peculiar place in the respect and even the affection of the American people; a place reached unconsciously and that cannot be resigned."

Unaware until then how critically ill he really was, the public was shocked by newspaper pictures of Taft being moved by wheel chair through Washington's Union Station. President Hoover visited him at home the next day, but after that he was allowed no visitors. Patrolmen were stationed along the walks near his home to maintain quiet, and twice-daily medical bulletins were issued from the White House for nearly a month. They reported that he had very high blood pressure, associated with general hardening of the arteries, a chronic cystitis, and inflammation of the muscles of the heart. Some days they reported him slightly improved, but Nellie was told privately that there was no hope and that he would slowly grow weaker.

He suffered no pain. At times, he was able to sit in a chair half the day. There were moments when his mind was clear, when he was pleased by the messages of respect read to him. His brothers and his sons visited and his daughter came to the house to stay. The long vigil went on, and it became the nation's.

What pleased him most was a letter read to him on February 14, from his fellow justices of the Supreme Court. Written by Holmes, for all the others to sign, it addressed Taft as "Mr. Chief Justice," and explained:

"We call you Chief Justice still—for we cannot give up the title by which we have known you all these later years and which you have made dear to us. We cannot let you leave us without trying to tell you how dear you have made it. You came to us from achievements in other fields and with prestige of the illustrious place that you lately had held and you showed us in new forms your voluminous capacity for getting work done, your humor that smoothed the tough places, your golden heart that brought you love from every side and most of all from your brethren whose tasks you have made happy and light. We grieve at your illness, but your spirit has given life an impulse that will abide whether you are with us or away."

Justice Holmes celebrated his own eighty-ninth birthday on Saturday, March 8, 1930. In fine spirits, Holmes good-naturedly joked with reporters and photographers, and then went into the Supreme Court chambers for conference on cases with the other justices. On his way to the Capitol to join them, Justice Edward Sanford stopped at his dentist's office to have an ulcerated tooth pulled. Sanford got up from the dental chair, felt dizzy, and collapsed to the floor unconscious. He was dead of internal poisoning a few hours later. The shocked justices were still discussing the news of Sanford's death when word reached them that same evening that Taft had died. Holmes, looking years older than he had that birthday morning, told reporters that "the late Chief Justice has found relief from his hopeless illness in death."

Nellie was with Taft in his room when he lapsed into the peaceful sleep from which he never awoke. When President Hoover was informed, he went immediately to the Taft home. Chief Justice Hughes and others soon arrived to give the family what personal help they could. Messages from presidents, kings and prime ministers, from governors, judges, and the world's other celebrated men, many of whom Taft had known, came to the White House offices that were kept open through the night.

President Hoover issued a proclamation for thirty days of national mourning. The Senate and House adjourned until after the funeral, as did many state legislatures, as well as the Supreme Court, where a seat was draped in black. Government, state and civic buildings were ordered closed, the New York Stock Exchange and commodity markets shut down, and thousands of private stores and offices suspended business. In New York one million school children took part in memorial exercises, and in hundreds of other schools children bowed their heads for periods of silence. Churches and universities held special services, and in London, Paris, Berlin, Tokyo and other capitals there were tributes.

In a pouring rain on Tuesday morning, March 11, long lines of people formed across the Capitol Plaza, and ten thousand people filed past Taft's coffin during the two hours that it lay in the Capitol rotunda, beneath the great dome on a catafalque upon which had rested the coffins of Lincoln, Garfield, McKinley and Harding. Dressed in his robes of office as Chief Justice, surrounded by military guards, he was the first former President who had not died in office to be so honored. Not far from the coffin was his old Supreme Court room, and closer there was a plaster model of his new Supreme Court building, a replica that had been put on display in the rotunda weeks before and now was banked with flowers.

At noon, the passing lines of people were halted and as the Marine Band softly played, the coffin was carried down the broad Capitol steps to a gun caisson harnessed to eight gray horses. Led by military units of soldiers, sailors and marines, the procession moved at a slow cadence for more than two hours through streets crowded with thousands who stood silent in the rain. At All Souls Unitarian Church, another dense crowd stood behind troops who lined the approach.

Within the red brick and white-steepled church, for which Taft years before had laid the cornerstone, the services were simple, as he had asked. In the pews were President Hoover, Vice President Curtis, the cabinet and several former members of Taft's own cabinet, heads of government agencies, Senators and Representatives, and those who had been closest to him, his Court family of justices and his own family: Nellie, his sons and daughter, his grandchildren, his brothers, and forty Taft relatives.

But there were no eulogies or sermons of praise. He had wanted none. The organ played and the steeple chimes echoed as two of his favorite hymns were sung. The Reverend Ulysses G. Pierce, who had been Taft's pastor and friend since he was Secretary of War, read from the Bible and from two poems Taft had liked. There was the benediction, and then the nine hundred friends who had filled the church moved outside, where the rain had stopped.

At Arlington National Cemetary, where Taft was the first former President to be buried, the services again were simple. President Hoover stood back to one side, the justices of the Supreme Court at the other, and Nellie and Taft's children close to the grave, flanked by soldiers. The Reverend Pierce read from the Bible, and then from Tennyson's "Crossing the Bar," another favorite poem of Taft's:

> Twilight and evening bell,
>   And after that the dark!
> And may there be no sadness of farewell,
>   When I embark.

Three sharp bursts of rifle fire broke the silence. A bugler played taps. The nation's only President and Chief Justice was lowered to his final resting place in the long sloping hillside across the river from the Capitol he loved.

Some Other Books About William Howard Taft

Butt, Archie, *Taft and Roosevelt: The Intimate Letters of Archie Butt,* Doubleday, Doran & Co., Inc., Garden City, N.Y., 1930.

Cotton, Edward H., *William Howard Taft, A Character Study,* The Beacon Press, Boston, 1932.

Duffy, Herbert S., *William Howard Taft,* Minton, Balch & Co., New York, 1930.

Hicks, Frederick C., *William Howard Taft, Yale Professor of Law and New Haven Citizen,* Yale University Press, New Haven, 1945.

McHale, Francis, *The Life and Public Services of William Howard Taft,* Dorrance & Company, Philadelphia, 1931.

Mason, Alpheus Thomas, *William Howard Taft; Chief Justice,* Simon & Schuster, New York, 1964.

Pringle, Henry F., *The Life and Times of William Howard Taft,* Holt, Rinehart and Winston, Inc., 1939.

Ragan, Allen E., *Chief Justice Taft,* Ohio State Archaelogical & Historical Society, Columbus, Ohio, 1938.

Ross, Ishbel, *An American Family, The Tafts,* The World Publishing Company, New York, 1964.

Taft, Mrs. William H., *Recollections of Full Years,* Dodd, Mead & Co., New York, 1914.

Wilensky, Norman M., *Conservatives in The Progressive Era, The Taft Republicans of 1912,* University of Florida Press, Gainesville, 1965.

INDEX